BLESSED TO BE
UNWANTED

BLESSED TO BE UNWANTED

CANDACE WEBB-HENDERSON

Angels Paradigm House
Los Angeles • Pittsburgh • Danville

Angels Paradigm House—First Edition, 2017
Printed in the United States of America
This book is based on a true story; the intention of the writer is to
inspire both children who feel or have felt abandoned and loss as well
as to acknowledge loving foster or adoptive parents. The characters
depicted here are based on actual persons, living or dead. The author
of this book does not dispense medical or psychological advice nor
recommend the use of any specific technique as a form of treatment for
physical or emotional conditions. Any attempt to treat or diagnose an
illness should come under the direction of a medical professional.

Library of Congress Cataloging-in-Publication Data
Webb-Henderson, Candace

Blessed to Be Unwanted: a legacy / by Candace Webb-Henderson.
—First Edition

ISBN 978-0-692-84227-0

Cover design by Kathi Dunn, www.dunn-design.com
Interior design by Dorie McClelland, www.springbookdesign.com
Logo design by Holly Hodson, www.amberbluemedia.com
Edited by: Mara Melton, www.maramelton.com
Author photo: Kimberly Ogden, kim@kimberlyogden.com

Dedication

I dedicate *Blessed to Be Unwanted* to my beloved mother Joan Doyle Webb, for you were and will always be my inspiration.

To all the babies and children of the world who may have been offered up for adoption or placed in foster homes, may each of you find your blessings in life and live your dreams much like my mother, grandmother, and grandfather did.

In loving memory
of my mother Joan Doyle Webb and
my beloved grandparents Frank and Dorothy Doyle

Contents

Foreword

The pain of a mother who knows she couldn't feed or care for her baby burst my heart open and tears poured down my cheeks as I read Iva's story. So many mothers have faced this dilemma; what can you do, give your precious baby to a stranger? That is just what Iva did when she handed her five-day-old baby to Dorothy and Frank for "temporary care."

And what about those babies; millions of children experience feeling alone, unwanted, and abandoned whether they are relinquished or stay with struggling families. Were you one of those children?

In 2015, the foster care system in the United States served 670,000 children, of those, 135,000 eventually went through the adoption process. *Blessed to Be Unwanted* offers inspiration and hope to readers of all ages who have felt alone, abandoned, or unwanted.

Iva's baby was Candace Henderson's mother. Baby Joni was blessed in that she grew up in a loving home. Joni's new parents, Dorothy and Frank, took care of 28 babies and toddlers all at once during World War II, including baby Joni. Just the thought of the amount of cloth diapers there was to wash on a daily basis is overwhelming. Dorothy's generosity and love for children taught her granddaughter Candace, "Every child matters, every life matters, foster parents who bring a child into their home can make all the difference in the world throughout generations to come by making them feel loved and not forgotten."

Very little has changed since 1936 when baby Joni was given to the Doyle's; currently, approximately 40,000 infants are placed in Foster Care each year. The Safe Haven, Child Abandonment law, has made it possible for mothers like Iva to place their babies in the care of strangers at fire stations, police stations, and hospitals. For some of the babies, adoption is a speedy process, while others may stay in the foster care system waiting for their families to return.

When we look with our hearts, not our eyes, unexpected acts of kindness, comfort, and love will appear. Dorothy raised Joni as her own daughter, teaching her to cook and clean, to care for others, to celebrate with gusto, and above all, to see through eyes of loving kindness. *Blessed to Be Unwanted* helps us to recognize those golden moments of goodness in our own lives. Perhaps you will be inspired to make a difference by teaching basic life skills to a child in need, or by making an effort to acknowledge the accomplishments of others.

As Joni grew, she saw the possibility of having a life that was worth living. Joni went on to find a loving husband and raise her two daughters with the continuing support of Grandma Dorothy and Grandpa Frank.

As with any good love story, this one extends beyond the grave, Dorothy had a keen intuition and knew that angels were always around guiding and nurturing her; Joni said, "Grandma Dorothy was her guardian angel." After Joni had passed, Candace wondered if her mom was her guardian and protector; of course, she was.

Angels come in many forms to guide us, comfort us, and protect us. Some are in human form like Grandma Dorothy offering kindness at just the right moment. Other angels work invisibly behind the scenes watching over us. I always felt loved and wanted by my parents. Sadly, it seems this is a rare blessing in this world; even so, there have been times in my life where I felt alone and abandoned. We all experience these moments, Dorothy and I have both experienced angels are the ones who show up for us with loving comfort, guidance, and protection. We all have guardian angels that have our best interests at heart. When we are attentive, we are able to see their influence through synergistic experiences, sudden inspiration, and brilliant ideas seem to pop out of nowhere.

Candace shows us how to access this type of love, which is available for all of us through life experiences. You can access it, too, by simply remembering a time when you felt deeply loved, and the love is there. Candace honored her mom Joni and her Grandma Dorothy by remembering the deep love they shared. *Blessed to Be Unwanted* teaches us to honor the love we have experienced in life; after all, love is the most powerful force in all of creation. Just as it did for Joni, your love prevails through challenges and triumphs over fears, grief, and loss. As you read, use this story to recognize your own journey of challenge and triumph. You have wisdom and kindness in your heart to share; you are valuable. The world is a better place because of you.

—Rev. Dr. Kimberly Marooney,
President of Gateway University,
Founder of The Angel Ministry,
Bestselling Author of *Angel Blessings Cards of Sacred Guidance and Inspiration* www.kimberlymarooney.com

Acknowledgments

I want to thank Peggy Anderson, an author and editor - thank you for taking the time to read my manuscript. I am thankful for meeting your daughter, of all places in Hawaii. It must have been fate, as I had been working on this book with my mother for years and never had the gumption to pass it along to anyone to read. Upon the completion of her critique, I could have admitted defeat; your encouragement helped me to never give up.

To my design and layout team, Kathi Dunn, and Dorie McClelland, thank you for your help in designing the cover and layout. Your stunning design captures the very essence of the book!

To my editor, Mara Melton, thank you for your continued efforts and support, I would not have been able to bring my work to a successful completion if it weren't for your keen eye in assisting me in ensuring that my words flow, as well as my grammar. I am amazed at your dedication and your attention to detail! There is no doubt in my mind your commitment to seeing this process through comes from your past experience as a foster parent.

To my dear friend, and technical writer, Holly Blissit, thank you so much for taking the time to read my manuscript. Your "eagle eye" and attention to detail is a talent. I am grateful that you not only assisted in helping me edit my website, but you took the time out of your busy life to read this beautiful body of work.

To my graphic designer, Holly Hodson, thank you for your brilliant and personal logo. It depicts the love and admiration as it relates to my mother's life. I also want to thank you for your guidance in helping me with the launch of my book as well as my website. You did an amazing job! I feel super blessed that I worked with you on this amazing project!

To my husband, Steve, thank you for supporting and encouraging me to never give up; your faith in me is what has kept me going to forge on and complete this body of work. I am thankful you believed in me, and I had you in my corner pushing me to finish. Thank you for not just supporting me, but knowing I could complete this book. I love you!

To my children, Devin Doyle and Carly Joan, thank you, as you are the best things I have ever done in my life! You both have given me encouragement. My mom, your grandma, once said, "All I want for my kids is a better life than what I had." I want that for you as well; I love you both so much always and forever.

To my twin sister, Connie, thank you. I know it has not always been easy growing up as twins. It seemed that there was always so much expected from us to be alike, but we are definitely two unique individuals. We were so blessed to have the love and care we had from our mom and dad; may they rest in peace. As Mom used to say to us, "All I ever want is for my girls to be there for one another. Family is everything, and we might not come from a big one, but what we do have is mighty, and no one will have your back like your family." Much love sissy!

To my cousin, Ben, thank you for taking that wild adventure cross-country. I am grateful you took that trip all those years ago, as we may have never reconnected. We were so fortunate to have had the opportunity to get to know one another; I love you. Thank you for being a part of our family. Mom always felt lucky to have gotten to know you as Connie and I did. Special thanks, for helping me express your thoughts in this, as that was a piece of the puzzle she would be so proud to have been included in her story. Special thanks to your wife Joanne, one of my closest and dearest friends, who also helped in finding the missing pieces to both of you.

To my Auntie Barb, Mom's dearest and best friend forever, thank you for allowing me to pick your brain for some of the finer details of Mom's life; if there was anyone who knew her, it was certainly you. You may not be an aunt by blood, but you are our family. I will love you forever and always. Who you are is what makes you so unique, and you were always there for Mom; thank you. I love you!

I would like to thank my mom, Joan Doyle Webb, it has been a journey, to say the least, in finding the right words to express all the wisdom, love, and support you have given me over the years. I feel so blessed to have been your daughter; I hope for years to come that I will prove to be as good a mother to Devin and Carly as you were to me. I love you, Mommy, always and forever.

To my Grandma Doyle thank you for being such a caring and loving mother and grandmother, you will be remembered and deeply missed forever. You were generous and kind to all those people that had the incredible fortune of meeting you. You were caring and understanding; you went to great lengths to reach out and help those in need. You had the ability to take whatever life dealt you and make the best of it in any given situation. Your selflessness in taking in so many children out of pure compassion makes you a hero in my book. Most importantly, what made you such an amazing person is you took in my mom and loved her throughout her life just as if she was your own. Thank you will never be enough.

Introduction

Over a hundred and thirty-five thousand babies are given up for adoption each year in the United States. It's hard to fathom that a significant proportion of children who enter the foster care system, come from international agencies, whereas only a small percentage of children from the United States are voluntarily relinquished to the foster care system or given up for adoption. In preparing to write this book I began to research foster care and adoption in the United States. What I discovered is that two of the most common feelings adopted children experience is rejection and abandonment, followed by grief and loss. It is impossible to predict when these feelings will appear or the behaviors associated with them; however, the research points out, it does occur at some point in their lives. Adopted children tend to think something is wrong with them because they were "unwanted."

During the process of writing this book, I met Monica Kelsey who was abandoned at birth. Monica founded Safe Haven Baby Boxes, and has made it her mission to educate others on the Safe Haven Law assisting women faced with the dilemma of an unexpected pregnancy. Although these women love their unborn children, she believes these baby boxes will ultimately help save the lives of innocent children. Safe Haven Baby Boxes allows a mother to place her child in a box that is fully equipped with heating and cooling along with an ADT system that notifies someone within 30 seconds there is a newborn placed in the box.

Blessed to Be Unwanted was deeply inspired by my mother, Joan Doyle Webb, who began to gather the information for the body of this work a few years before her passing. She believed she was blessed in every way because her mother gave her to the Doyle's to be cared for and raised. Like many, she too experienced fear as a child, but her legacy began with a brave, loving woman who, with her husband took her in, from a street corner when she was just five days old. My grandparents, Dorothy and Frank, brought her to their home; they fell in love with her from the moment they laid eyes on her. My grandparents also took care of twenty-eight other children during and after World War II.

As a mother, I cannot imagine what it must have been like for Mom's biological mother, Iva, to leave her with perfect strangers. It is now clear to me; that it was Mother's destiny to be raised and loved by the Doyle's; I shudder to think how much she would have suffered otherwise. Child abandonment often leads to the child having feelings of rejection. I believe my mom's intention was to offer hope to those who experience this. It was her hope they would seek their life's passion with eagerness and fervor, and make a difference just by living life to the fullest, much as she did. It was her greatest wish to continue her foster mother's legacy and her love for humanity in the form of a book, dedicated to the children of the world who have been given up for adoption regardless of the circumstances. *Blessed to Be Unwanted* is a real account and testament to every life. It has purpose and meaning and is relevant to the value found in everyone regardless of what country you came from, your race, or social status. It is a reminder for all of us to see how one couple changed the course of a child's life and led to this legacy of two generations of loving families. Dorothy and Frank's deep love for one another and for Joni runs through my veins and my childrens' as well; and will thread through the lives of many generations to come.

Thank you, Mom, for giving me the honor to share your story, for I too, received a blessing for having YOU as my mother.

Chapter 1

The Hand Off

She handed over her five-day-old baby to a woman she had never met before on a street corner in Wilkinsburg, Pennsylvania. Dorothy took her into her arms, held the baby close to her heart, and wondered if this precious infant would ever see her mother, Iva again. She hoped this mother would reclaim her child soon. The year was 1936 and times were challenging for single moms, particularly for Iva who had five children out of wedlock.

Just hours before, the phone rang, the buzzing sound shook Dorothy right out of her chair; she quickly jumped to her feet and answered the phone,

"Hello," there was a bit of a pause, "Hello is anyone there?"

She could hear breathing; with some hesitation, a woman answered with a quivering tone, "Hello is this Dorothy Doyle?" She didn't recognize the lady's voice and answered, "Why yes this is she, how can I help you?"

"My name is Iva Goulding, and I am anxious to find someone to help me with my newborn. It is my understanding that you take in children to watch after. I got your name from the Rosalia Center. I only want to leave my daughter with you for a short time, just until I get on my feet, and I can care for her myself."

Dorothy's loving husband, Frank, was more than just a bit leery about the phone call, as this lady seemed to have no idea when she would be coming back for her daughter. He knew in his heart taking in this child would be different from the way the other kids had come to be with them. He also realized his wife could never turn her back on a child in need. She pleaded with him, "How can we say no to this woman? She needs us, and the baby deserves a good home!" He was concerned not knowing anything about her but was sympathetic for the baby's sake. Frank felt the attachment Dorothy would form with this baby, and this worried him for whenever Iva might come back for her.

"Let's just say if I agree with this notion of taking in this little girl, did she tell you why she couldn't take care of her?"

Dorothy responded with conviction in her voice, "I have to go by her word she is struggling financially and needs our help until she can save up enough money to land on her feet. This mother promised she would return and I have to believe her."

Frank then agreed, "OK . . . ok . . . ok, what did you say her name was?"

She stared brazenly into his eyes and said, "Iva, Iva Goulding."

"Well did she happen to tell you the baby's name?"

She was getting irritated with all of the questionings, and she angrily blurted out, "No! She didn't, and it shouldn't matter because the baby needs us."

Frank finally gave in. He then wrapped his arms around her and replied, "Call Iva back and tell her we will take the baby and care for her until she is able." Dorothy tightly wrapped her arms around him and began kissing him all over his face with such happiness; she was overjoyed with excitement and could hardly contain herself as she called Iva back.

Dorothy did not hear the phone ring on her end, "Iva, this is Dor-"

Before she could get the rest of her words out, Iva quickly reacted, "Well, what did your husband say, can you take my daughter for me?"

Without hesitation, she answered, "Yes, of course, we are happy to take your little one, and we will take care of her if you need our help."

Tears of relief overcame Iva with joy as she was relieved knowing her baby would be taken in by the Doyle's and well cared for; "I was hoping you could meet me, as I am not all that familiar with Wilkinsburg."

This new momma had never met them and yet was still willing to hand her newborn over to them. Can you possibly imagine leaving your brand-new infant with a perfect stranger? It is incomprehensible to think that is just what this woman was proposing but by the sound of things, she was desperate to find a home for her daughter. That baby was my mother.

That day, Frank and Dorothy drove to where they were to meet Iva. When they arrived, a young woman was waiting with a baby in her arms beside an old Packard sedan parked on the corner of Main Street. As they approached her, Dorothy immediately recognized her voice. She was alone, and she looked scared. Along with the baby was $5.00 tucked in a beautiful pink blanket. She spoke in a brittle tone trying to hold back her tears, "I am ever so grateful for your help; I don't even have the words to express my gratitude. I am not married, and the father doesn't know; he can't because he is married. I ran away to Pittsburgh to have her, and as you can imagine, this would dishonor my family."

Dorothy stared into Iva's eyes compassionately; she wanted her to feel at ease. She thoughtfully reassured Iva, "I can only imagine the pain you are feeling to give up your baby but you can be free from worry, we will love her as if she were our own."

Iva began to weep as she placed her newborn into Dorothy's arms. Iva cried, "Please call her Joan Helen. I like Joni. She looks like a Joni, don't you think?"

As she handed her over, Dorothy comforted her, "Joni, what a lovely name for such a cute baby girl, we will love and cherish each day she is with us."

Dorothy looked at Frank to gain his approval who said, "Yes, absolutely we will." Of course, we will take excellent care of your daughter until you are ready to come back for her."

Iva then wiped the tears from her face and kissed Joni on her forehead, "Goodbye my dear Joni; goodbye for now. I will be back for you very soon, I promise!"

Dorothy was doing her best to reassure her, Joni was in the best of hands. It appeared the longer she lingered over the baby, the more Iva seemed to have second thoughts.

Dorothy declared, "Please don't worry about her, you can call anytime." It was not long before Iva started to turn away and walk towards the car. Dorothy and Frank stood on the street corner and watched as Iva left.

She then turned around and shouted, "Take good care of my little girl, I am sorry, mommy must leave you, for now, I will be back for you, I love you!"

As Iva got in the car and waved goodbye, Frank and Dorothy wondered if this woman would ever return for her child. Dorothy believed the woman's story; Frank, on the other hand, was not as sure. While she drove away that day, Frank made a mental note of her license plate number; later this would become the only link to identify her. Dorothy looked down at Joni, and her eyes filled up with tears. She looked so peaceful and calm and had no idea her biological mother just handed her off to perfect strangers.

The couple arrived home with their newest addition. For my

grandparents, this was an extraordinary moment, it was like an early birthday gift as this little bundle of joy came to Dorothy just one day before her birthday. My grandmother reflected that Joni was the prettiest baby girl ever, with olive tone complexion, black curly hair, and dark eyes. She probably weighed a little over 8 lbs. They didn't get much rest as it was, with all the other children they cared for during the daytime, and now they were going to have to get used to the nightly feedings and diaper changes. It was evident from Frank's smile that cracked his face how overjoyed he was, as he typically hid his feelings. It spread from his tightly pressed mouth, past his round rosy-red cheeks all the way to his hairline. Grandma used to say he was like a kid in a candy store.

As much as Joni became a birthday gift to Dorothy, in return, it was the greatest gift she could ever hope for by being placed in the arms of this sweet and loving couple. Frank was not very religious, but if there was ever a time when he believed in God, it was now, as he felt God placed this precious child in his life through fate.

Joni was now living among the flock of babies Dorothy had taken in over several months as a foster mother. The children varied in ages, and their parents came from all different backgrounds. No one ever called or checked in on Joni's well-being, unlike the other kids, and no one came back for her either; Frank turned out to be right about her biological mother after all.

There was no way to know at the time that Dorothy would become this precious little girl's actual mother. I know Grandma became my mom's true mother in every sense of the word, the minute she took her in her arms. Joni felt the love and devotion my grandparents showed her and this was a blessing despite being abandoned, by definition. They wanted her when no one else did, and she became their little girl. I will forever be grateful for that moment because had Dorothy not taken her on that day, she would never have become my grandma Dorothy.

I did not grow up in the sense of having my grandmother near me. The distance between our families made it difficult to have a regular and meaningful relationship with her. Back in the days when talking on the phone was a luxury due to the cost, calls were prearranged and made on a weekly basis. Mom typically called Grandma once a week to check in on her. Some of my fondest memories of visiting Grandma Dorothy in that big house will always be in my mind. I loved staying with Grandma and chatting with her mysterious tenants; her home was like living in a castle. Frank and Dorothy lived in the basement, as did my mom when she was growing up in this seventeen-room boarding house. The basement was by no means luxurious; the floors and the perimeter of the walls were all made of stone, the carpet was not plush under their feet. During the winter months, the floor would get cold, and Grandma would buy rugs on sale; it didn't matter if they matched, the goal was to scatter them throughout the basement to keep the children's feet warm.

When we visited, the chilly air wrapped around my sister and I like a coat of armor, as we ascended the curved staircase to the foyer. In this shadowed darkness, our ears were on high alert, as well as our senses. It was as if we were looking for ghosts and whatever else we might encounter there. Our feet made it to the main floor where the focal point was the staircase made of black carved Teak wood. When stepping onto the stairs, our eyes would seek the light shining through the panoramic colored glass window; it was my mom's favorite. It added such beauty and illumination that it inspired anyone who had the fortune of seeing it. This magnificent piece of glass hangs in my house today, and it will forever remind me of my grandma. I just love it so!

My sister and I slept in a small room in the basement off the kitchen. I recall a time when we were building a tent with a blanket and a stick we placed upright in the middle of the bed. We were supposed to be sleeping, but Connie and I were giggling, trying to be quiet. Through the window above our bed, we heard all sorts of strange noises; the sound of the wind whistling through the branches of the trees, the rise, and fall of conversations in the nearby alley, and cars whizzing by on the street. On one evening, my sister and I were restless, so we started jumping on the bed. Connie fell and split her chin on the corner of the frame.

"Oh, nooo!" I screamed.

She began crying, her words stuttering as she tried to speak. Tears were running down her cheeks, and the blood oozed from her face. We were guaranteed a tongue-lashing, regardless of who heard us. Grandma heard the ruckus and quickly pushed her way into the bedroom, shrieking, "What is going on in here? You girls are supposed to be sleeping!"

Connie was in a panic, "I fell, and hurt myself."

She rushed her into the kitchen so she could get a better look; there was no question she was mad at us from the harsh tone of her voice. She grabbed a wet towel and dabbed away the blood.

In a firm and assuring tone, my Grandmother said, "Settle down, you are going to be fine."

Connie continued to sob with a lump in her throat. "I'm sorry, I'm sorry, am I going to have to get stitches?"

"Calm down now; I don't think your chin is stitch worthy, I just need to clean it up and get a bandage on it." Even though she was stern with us, I knew she loved us. It was also important for me to keep my mouth shut while I watched Grandma tend to Connie. I knew better than to say anything at that moment.

"Now off to bed, and no horsing around, you hear!" Grandma instructed.

We whimpered, and said, "Goodnight," in unison.

With that, we jumped into bed, closed our eyes, and called it a day. Grandma lived through the Great Depression; she was always worried she could fall on hard times. I recall as a little girl finding a coffee can with a roll of money in it. My sister and I were in awe. We couldn't believe how big the roll of cash was; in fact, we would sometimes sneak the coffee can into our bedroom and try to count it. Our eyes almost fell out of our heads, when we calculated approximately $5,000. It wasn't until years later we found out she stashed several cans throughout the basement. Stashing cash, was Grandma's way of feeling safe and assuring that she would have enough money in case of an emergency.

Our little hearts would pound as we cautiously made our way up into her giant house. Connie and I used to slither up the stairs with a bit of darkness that loomed in the basement from the cellar doors all the way up to the first floor. When we reached the top, we could secretly get a glimpse of some of the tenants. The home where my mother grew up seemed so big to my sister and me. Our footsteps creaked on the wooden stairs. We laughed wondering if there would be someone lurking inside the old house as we finally reached the top. What a remarkable sight as we slowly peeked around the corner to catch sight of the hallway that stretched beyond, overlooking the massive front porch. Without pause, we pushed our way towards the front door. I can only imagine how my mom felt growing up in this big house!

I faintly remember a brass plated inlay marker apparently representing the Greek Consulate. To our family and the renters, being outside was a joy for socializing and getting to know one another. All around the porch were vines of beautiful morning glories. Oh, how gorgeous those morning glories grew to be! They were all different colors from blue, pink, purple to red! Her roses were another one of my favorites. Like an artist with a palette, she lined the front entryway in all different colors with them.

Then, there was the smell of the flowers, which pleasantly traveled through our nostrils and I must tell you, the scent was heavenly. I loved the porch swings, the comfortable patio couches, and the many wooden rockers. Every morning seemed like a picturesque morning because you could see folks enjoying themselves with their coffee and paper. The best part for my sister and I was swaying back and forth relaxing and enjoying our sweet tea.

It was such a treat spending time outside with my sister and my mom. We used to love hanging out together. Learning how to play solitaire at a very young age with Grandma was loads of fun. She had such a passion for the game; she had a deck of cards she enjoyed the most. Remarkably, although worn out and faded after so much use over the years, I still have those cards. I am so grateful Mom saved them as a precious memento of one of her favorite hobbies.

I remember how it used to tickle me when Grandma would sit at the table while shuffling and say, "Baby, it all depends on the first hand, and I can tell whether I have a good hand."

I would watch and often wonder what she meant, and asked, "What are you saying you know, how can you tell?"

She would say, "Oh I can just feel it in my bones."

Sure enough, her intuition was right on the money as she turned over the first cards to determine her winning hand. Playing solitaire was also one of my mother's much-loved pastimes. We played all sorts of different board games. Some of the games she taught us that we enjoyed playing were Tic-Tac-Toe and Checkers.

My grandma passed away in 1991, with her daughter, my mom, by her side all the way to the end. They talked a little during that time and surprisingly, she was aware of everything around her. When she died, Grandma was reassured, when she got a visit from Frank, who had passed away in 1960; he was waiting for her. Grandma and Mom believed in angels and up until my mom's death, she would say that Grandma was her "Guardian Angel." Minutes after my mom passed away, I thought to myself, "Would my mother be our protector, watching over my sister and me?" I am confident the gates of heaven opened to receive my mom and my grandmother because their faith was so undeniably pure.

Grandma and Our Past Generations

Traveling through the scenic meadows of western Pennsylvania, there are several small boroughs, Harmony, Zelienople, Connoquenessing, and finally Evans City, approximately 25–30 miles from Pittsburgh. Driving into Evans City, is the official welcome sign; under it, are the words, "The City of Black and Gold," because of the oil discovered in 1915, and out of that, this small town grew up around all the oil production. Oil derricks sprouted up all over in many backyards throughout the village. The oil enthusiasm only lasted a couple of years, but this discovery created wealth for people throughout this area. I still picture driving from Illinois to Pennsylvania beneath a canopy of crimson leaves, my sister and me lying on the back of the station wagon, ranting, "Are we there yet, how much longer?" It made my parents crazy; we sounded like a broken record repeating ourselves every fifteen minutes. It was so thrilling for us when we saw the sign because we knew we were almost there.

There was a sign marking a quaint valley surrounded by large hills and a lovely landscape, which is home to the horror film cult classic *Night of the Living Dead.* The Evans City Cemetery Chapel is featured in the film's opening scene. One of the many people who came by to enjoy the comforts of Grandma's enticing front porch was the director of the film, along with his wife. They lived next door to Grandma's boarding house. They visited with her discussing all sorts of topics including the stock market. Although Grandma had a trusted broker for years, it was important to her to stay educated on the subject. After all, she was not in the stock market to lose money; making money was something she took quite seriously.

Many of the conversations the famous cult classic director had with my grandma were about his film. He found out she had a family resort, not too far from the cemetery. With her permission, he shot a couple of scenes on the grounds of her Wonderland Park home. She not only befriended a famous movie director, but she was related to the actor, Mr. Raymond Burr. When I look at pictures of him, I can see a slight resemblance to Dorothy as a young woman; this is where she grew up. Before my mother passed away, she wanted me to make sure to include Dorothy's story and the loving, kind, woman she was to all. She touched everyone she knew, especially my mom and all the children she cared for, at a time when so many mothers needed a helping hand. From my experience, I remember her nurturing ways. She sacrificed her career as a nurse to care for the many children in need, including my mom.

Dorothy was born on March 6, 1903, the oldest of five children to Phillip and Mae Burr who were tenant farmers; they didn't have much, but there was always food on the table. She had several brothers and a sister. Her oldest brother, Phillip, died at a very young age; losing her brother was difficult for her as well as her mother. The loss of a child is probably the most devastating experience for a parent to endure. She knew she would have to be strong for her mother.

In the small town of Connoquenessing, my great-great grandfather founded a small Lutheran church. Many generations of the Burr family were born and raised there; parents raised their children in the church, and the children had their weddings in that church. The family cemetery is there, many of our family members who have passed are buried there; Phillip is laid to rest there as well.

Connoquenessing is a typical small town where everyone knew each other and each other's business as well. The town was home to many families of German descent. One of our family traditions for generations was to place flowers on all the family graves before Memorial Day. Planting flowers is a tradition our family still follows today. I always wondered about the superstition of, "Step on a crack and break your mother's back." Many people never knew the origin of the saying. Grandma told my mom, if you stepped on the graves, it would bring you bad luck. My mother told my sister and me the same story, and anytime we visited a cemetery we made sure we did not step on any of the burial plots. Avoiding stepping on the gravesites was just one of the family customs that was passed down throughout generations. Family traditions are unique; it is important to carry them on as it facilitates not only high family values but high personal values as well. I feel fortunate I grew up in a tiny town, as it helped form who I am today.

It is quite common in a small town for people to be caught up in each other's business. I grew up in a small rural area, Danville, Illinois, and I can remember the gossiping that went on all over town as well as people judging one another. It seems more of this goes down in smaller communities than the big city, but I am sure the crime is much higher in larger cities as well. One thing for certain, you could knock on your neighbors' door and ask for just about anything you needed. Let me just say "in my day" whenever you borrowed a couple of eggs, not only did you replace the eggs, but you handed them a plate of the cookies the eggs were used in. I long for those nostalgic times and friendly neighbors.

Those days, meals were always made very special. Even though both of my parents worked, we managed to make time for supper at the table every day. I can picture myself at Grandma's having Sunday night dinners. There is something to be said about the Sunday dinners; one of my favorite memories growing up was Grandma's homemade noodles and chicken soup along with her homemade ice cream for dessert.

Her mother Mae, my great grandmother, had relatives living in Pittsburgh; they lived a much easier life. She dreamed of the day that her children would lead a more comfortable and better existence. Despite their hardships, she raised her kids to value education and to be strong. It is especially evident with Grandma because going to school was important to her; she attended a small one-room schoolhouse. It reminded me of growing up on "Little House on the Prairie." Old report cards showed she received all "A's," and per her teacher, was well ahead of her classmates.

I can only imagine her excitement of getting into the nursing program. I guess this trait was passed down to Grandma and Mom, as they both aspired to one day go to nursing school. Grandmother attended her training at Passavant Hospital in Pittsburgh, which was run by the Lutherans. It was also an honor to have received a glowing letter of recommendation from her minister. Her high grades paid off; the nursing program she applied to accepted her and she was now on her way to fulfilling her dream of making a better life for herself and her family. There was a point in my life where I too thought I would become a nurse and follow in my mother's and grandmother's footsteps, but destiny had different plans for me.

Grandma did not take nursing school lightly; I can completely understand, she had a mission: her primary goal was to finish school and get a good-paying job to help support her family financially. When she graduated, her mother Mae placed an extraordinary note behind her diploma, which read:

Dorothy as a young nursing student

My Dorothy, perhaps you will find this someday. The date is September 14, 1929, at 4613 Center Avenue, Pittsburgh, PA. I am framing your R.N. diploma as my one prized possession. I am proud of you, my dear. I'm putting this note in as I put the back cover on the frame. I wonder when you will find it. I will carry with me the love I feel for you when I go to meet our dear ones gone before me. I will take care of the other children until you come to me and I'll be watching for each one of you to be as I have one who reveres God. —Mother

This letter must have been very special to my grandma and mother. My mom had it tucked away in her diary for years. The note, written in pencil, was very fragile after all these years.

Grandmother found her first well-paying job as a private duty Registered Nurse. Initially, she worked for a very well-to-do family, whose son, Clarence, was a paraplegic, injured in a tragic auto accident. At the time, private duty nursing paid the highest salaries; only the most affluent could afford to pay for this type of care. Her hours were long and she typically only got one day off each week. Even as a young woman, her heart was enormous; due to the poverty she was born into, she found it gratifying to helping others. Her eagerness to make a difference coupled with her work ethic gave her a tremendous sense of confidence and happiness. Grandma was happy because she was finally able to earn enough money to support her family. She was employed by the same household for a decade and always had nothing but good memories of the experience. Mom always told me how happy Grandmother was because Clarence and his relatives treated her so well.

From a very early age, my mom enforced if you want something out of life you must put forth the effort. She used to shop at K-Mart, as that's all they could afford. Connie and I always dressed alike, and we were getting sick of it; we are fraternal twins. Mother did not mince words as she informed us nicer clothes are costly, which only meant, "get a job to earn your money." Neither one of us was afraid to work; with a little nudge and some guidance, we were working in no time. My uncle managed corn fields; as a side job during the summer months, he helped us get our first job detasseling corn. Detasseling corn is labor intensive; children of the corn could have been our nickname, as we were kids that walked the cornfields for miles pulling the tops off the corn. Because of that experience, I now have the greatest appreciation for the high school students who trudge through the muddy fields during the hot, humid months to ensure we get to eat delicious sweet corn. Mom said the work was extremely demanding but well worth it. What we learned from my mom and grandmother was a strong work ethic and compassion; I feel blessed, as these qualities have been passed on to my children.

Over the years, Grandma spent long hours, day after day with Clarence; over time, he developed a strong affection for her. He bought her a one-carat diamond ring. At the time, she considered this gift a bit extravagant and refused to accept it from him. He confessed that he merely wanted to show his appreciation for her taking care of him.

When she opened the box, her immediate response was, "How lovely, but this is far too expensive, and I can't accept it. You have to take it back."

Clarence sensed her desire to give it back, so he blurted, "No! You aren't going to return this gift, if you do, you will make me heartbroken!"

The last thing she wanted to do was to make him sad. At the same time, she knew it cost him a lot of money, and she worried he wanted more than just her caregiving.

He began to rationalize why he chose a diamond ring, "It's not at all what you think, and I am not expecting anything from you, other than taking care of me as you do. It brings me happiness to be able to give you something, and I want you to remember our friendship, that is all." He would not take "no" for an answer. Insistently, he told her to wear it and enjoy it!

Grandma eventually succumbed and accepted the gift. Unbe-knownst to her at the time, she would one day give that same diamond to her loving husband, and the gem became an heirloom. She had it set in a thick platinum band, surrounded by 18 karat gold chunks on each side. Grandma cherished it for years, and it was passed on to my mom and dad. My mother's wish upon her death was to leave it to her first-born grandson, Devin Doyle. He will wear the ring once he marries. As a family superstition, once he puts the ring on, he cannot take it off; if he does, the luck will pour out of it.

Grandma was now living in Oakland, Pennsylvania, in a rooming house where she lived on the second floor and shared a bathroom with three other tenants. Her rent was thirty dollars per month. Back in those days, thirty dollars was a lot of money; today that will not even get you enough groceries to last a couple of days.

To ensure she was never late to work she would wake up one hour earlier in the morning before the others. Imagine having to share a bathroom with three others whom you don't know and trying to coordinate bathroom schedules.

Grandma liked to keep a spick-and-span house. Good bathroom etiquette was essential to her; she would take a few easy measures to ensure the comfort and benefit of anyone else. Respecting the others, she would make sure the toilet was flushed and kept the sink and tub clean. Per my grandmother's standards, there was nothing worse than walking into a bathroom and seeing someone else's strands of hair wrapped around a bar of soap or stuck to the drains. Grandma hoped by setting a good example and showing good restroom manners, her roommates would follow her lead, but someone always fell short. Soon it became apparent it was unlikely things would be kept clean but keeping the bathroom clean, was important to her.

I guess I am not the only one who is seemingly obsessed with keeping a clean house. I tend to stress out if my home isn't spotless. To me, there is no surprise as to where I got that trait! My mom was similar; she would have my sister and I tidy up daily. I find myself washing up behind my kids and husband, even after they have just cleaned. Today I have the same characteristic of ensuring we keep our home spotless, especially the washroom.

Sadly, Clarence became very ill; he was spending longer stays in the hospital. Since Clarence was a frequent patient in the hospital, there was no need for my grandmother to care for him as a full-time private duty nurse. She would still visit and sit with him often, but she did not expect him to compensate her. Dorothy soon realized it was time to look for alternative work. She

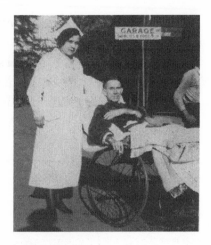

Dorothy and Clarence

applied at a nearby community hospital and began working part-time, which later became a full-time position as a bedside nurse. Dorothy finally ended her career as a private duty nurse.

Clarence soon passed away; Grandma took this very hard, nurses are taught to show empathy with their patients, and she took pride in attempting to understand the feelings of those she cared for and nurtured. I have always known nurses make a difference in the lives of those they care for, as my mom and grandmother did; they created a warm, comforting, and peaceful environment for their patients in their greatest time of need. Although the loss of Clarence deeply saddened her, she always had the wonderful memories they shared.

When Grandma began working, she sent money home to her family on a regular basis. When she started her new job, her two brothers Bill and George found work at the J&L Steel Mill, earning a very decent living. Her baby sister, Bernice, was so proud of her she too chose to pursue a career in nursing and trained at Shadyside Hospital.

It wasn't until I became an adult that I learned my Grandma Dorothy dreamed of owning and operating a cottage resort where wealthy city folk could find a retreat on the weekends and holidays to escape the long hot summers. My sense was her hard work finally had to pay off. As much as she wanted the time to relax, this was not an option until she had earned enough money to warrant slowing down.

To realize this dream, she first had to acquire the property. The endeavor became a family affair, as both of her brothers decided they wanted to be a part of the venture. She had a goal, and for most people, the hardest part of realizing the vision was to know what it was. As a little girl, I recall visiting the charming resort the Burr family worked so hard on to make a peaceful place for families to vacation.

Everything about the farmhouse as well as the cottages had a story to tell. You could see that the objects inside and outside of the farmhouse were well loved. Each time we visited, the pond would instantly grab my attention. There were all sorts of critters living amongst the lily pads: from frogs to goldfish, koi, ducks,

Farmhouse, early 1970s

and turtles. One of our favorite pastimes was to gather around the pond to get a glimpse of the wildlife.

At the front of the grounds, there was an old farmhouse perched atop a hill which became the home of Mae and her youngest brother, who set up housekeeping on the weekends and traveled to Pittsburgh to their rented efficiency apartment during the week. They left the little country home late Sunday evenings so Mae's youngest boy could work at the steel mill all week and return to the farmhouse on Friday.

Chapter 2

Frank and Dorothy's Love Story

In the meantime, Grandma also continued to live at the boarding house and work at the hospital. George and Dorothy worked the farmstead whenever they had time off from their primary jobs. She knew he was sacrificing spending time with his family; but in her mind the quicker the resort was completed, the sooner everyone could enjoy the fruits of their labor, along with their families. It was obvious to me while she was telling me about the resort that it just could not get done fast enough in her mind. George imagined his sister meeting a nice gentleman who would take care of her. By someone, I mean a man who would steal her heart and fill her life with all its simple pleasures in life.

Dorothy knew what to expect each morning and evening when she returned home until one day, someone unfamiliar entered her life. Everything in her life was about to change just as she was settling into a familiar routine. She was finally at ease with the people who lived on her floor.

A tall, redheaded Irishman moved into a room on the floor just above hers. I so wish I could have met him because through the years he was portrayed as a great father and husband. I can only imagine what a wonderful grandfather he would have been to Connie and me.

Three Irish Devils — Frank (middle) and his brothers

Daniel Francis Doyle was born on April 27, 1887. He went by the nickname, Frank. He was a salesman but dreamed of being a famous Irish tenor. He sang with his two brothers. They called themselves the "Three Irish Devils." In 1917, 1918, and several years after that, they were the headlining act in East Hampton, Massachusetts, at the Hampton Terrace Club in the Minstrels Theater. They sang every Wednesday and Thursday evening, and people came from all over to listen to their beautiful harmonizing voices. Grandpa had such a pleasant tone to his voice; he often sang solos.

He and his brothers dreamed of one day performing in New York City; unfortunately, before they could realize their dream, the country headed into the Great Depression, and they were forced to look for work. He found work at a company based in Massachusetts, which sent him to Pittsburgh as their lead sales-man working at a furnace company promoting gas.

I find it interesting that back in those days whiskey was hard to come by and cost more than he could afford. As necessity is the mother of invention, it made me chuckle when I learned my grandfather decided to construct a potato still in the closet of his boarding room to brew enough whiskey for his pleasure. He was so proud of the fact it saved him money, and he would not have to go out and buy it anymore.

One evening, the still overflowed, leaking through the floor-boards down into my grandmother's room below. This mishap facilitated his first memorable meeting with her. It was certainly not Frank's intent to cause any upset or damage to the apartment; however, I have to believe this was the beginning of his and Dorothy's life-long love affair.

While sitting in her apartment, Grandma noticed something leaking through her ceiling. She began to rant to herself, "What in the world is that smell, it smells like cheap whiskey!" She heard a dripping noise, and it sounded like it was coming through her ceiling. She looked up and saw a brownish liquid dribbling through the ceiling almost like tiny raindrops. She ran into the kitchen to get a pot to catch the oozing brownish liquid that was steadily falling, drip by drip into the pan. Her hands were shaking, and she could feel her blood pressure rise as she wondered how she would approach the person who lived above her. Grandma mustered up the courage to march up the stairs; she realized it was the new tenant. She curled her hand into an iron fist and pounded on his door. From the sounds of her knock, Frank envisioned a large person on the other side of the door; much to his surprise, it was a small but sturdy young lady glaring at him while chewing him out.

She didn't even introduce herself as she yelled and pointed her finger at him, "What is leaking through my floor boards? It sure smells like whiskey to me!" She then shoved her way through his door further yelling, "For heaven's sake, what is causing this leak?" I can only imagine the angst she must have felt; what an uncomfortable situation it must have been for her. I'm confident her heart was pounding with worry and how scared she probably felt, as she had no idea how he would react.

As a woman, I have no doubt she dreamt of someday meeting her soul mate. There's no feeling quite like meeting the person with whom you are supposed to spend the rest of your life. It just so happened for the two of them this was their rare and unusual moment; when their eyes locked, she and Frank felt a divine spark of light that connected their hearts forever.

The rooms were not very big; therefore, it did not take her very long to find the source. My mom reflected that Frank was speechless, as he could not get over what a total spitfire this little woman was! I remember my mom laughing as she told me the story.

Her words came out of her mouth like fiery ice. "I have lived here for some time, most of us live by one another, and I will not tolerate you or anyone else polluting this house with piss whiskey." He apologized profusely. Grandma was in shock; she could not believe he was distilling his whiskey. Frank sincerely and repeatedly kept saying, "I am sorry, I meant no harm, and I certainly did not mean for my alcohol to spill over and leak into the floor boards."

All Grandma cared about was the leaking to stop. Frank exclaimed, "I will clean up the mess, please calm down." Her blood was boiling and emotions running high, it was incredibly frustrating. I'm sure words flew from her mouth she never thought would. She got all up in his face! I know when my tensions are running high I tend to say things I might regret. I love the fact that Dorothy had the courage to challenge him, as she might not have ever fallen in love with him. Grandma was someone who had to get the last word. My mom always said the same thing about me; getting the last word is another trait I take from my grandma.

Grandma shouted, "By the looks of it, you are a grown man— old enough to know right from wrong and you should recognize how irresponsible this is! Not only could I tell the landlord but I could also inform the authorities, what do you think of that?"

Frank admitted to his wrongdoing and continued to apologize, "Again I am so sorry, words can't express how sorry I am." Then he looked into her sizzling eyes noticing a flickering of laughter emanating from them. At that moment, he knew he was attracted to her big blue eyes and soft brown colored curls. Then he narrowed in closer and said, "You never did tell me your name, let me be the first to introduce myself, my name is Frank Doyle."

She was speechless, and I think for the first time she was at a loss for words. Frank then offered her a glass of his whiskey in hopes this would assist in settling her down. She would have no part of sitting down with him and having a sip of whiskey because the only thing on her mind was getting the leak to stop.

Frank then explained, "I just discovered the unfortunate accident of my still overflowing, and before I could tend to clean up the spillage, you were at my door knocking."

Dorothy expressed, "I appreciate your offer to clean up the mess in my apartment, but not so sure I feel comfortable allowing you in my home. I don't even know you!"

Grandma began to compose herself, as Frank was in complete understanding of her being so upset.

She then introduced herself, "My name is Dorothy Burr," begrudgingly she accepted his apology.

Amid all the chaos and her yelling, Dorothy fascinated Frank. In fact, he found her to be irresistible, as she would further reprimand him with her subtle mumblings.

It was apparent his personality and charm began to soften her with compliments, "I admire your strong willed authoritative approach, not to mention how pretty you are."

She responded, "Thank you, but don't think your smooth talking is going to make up for your carelessness," while maintaining her composure.

Frank knew although this was an awkward incident, it was also an opportunity to use this catastrophic event to his advantage and ask Dorothy out on a date. Without hesitation, he asked her if she would have dinner with him. She was not so quick to accept his offer, but over the course of their conversation and his persuasion, she agreed to go out with him. I wasn't surprised to learn Grandma was less than accepting of this at first because she was a lady and in that era, a proper courtship was paramount.

Mom told me their first date was magical as Frank took her to the Phipps Conservatory and Botanical Gardens, which was in Oakland at Schenley Park. Steel Baron, Henry Phipps commissioned the greenhouse as a gift to the city in 1893. It is one of the nation's oldest and largest Victorian glass houses. Silver domes of glass covered the gardens. Thirteen different rooms were brimming with thousands of exotic plants and florets. Blossoms were always a part of Grandma's life. At the time, Frank had no idea she had a passion for flowers. He was already off to a great start. This trip was the first of many they would take together, hand in hand.

After their first date, Grandma became the object of Frank's adoration. He fell in love with her overnight. Though she enjoyed the time she spent with him, she was determined not to lose sight of her dream to own and manage a resort in the country. My grandfather knew this was important to her and the sacrifices she was making to fulfill her dream. Dorothy's tenacity was just one of the many qualities he saw in her.

As young or single women; we hope to find Mr. Right; much like my grandma, it was surprising to think I could find mine on a blind date. I think most would agree blind dates are typically taboo. An acquaintance of mine was insistent we meet. I wasn't very keen on going out with someone I had never met or had a conversation with. Well, I caved and decided to go. There was a knock on the door, and a voice spoke letting me know he was indeed my date. My heart began to flutter as I rechecked my outfit and my hair in the mirror.

The look on my face when we met in person is fixed in his mind forever, as my expression showed how stunned I was when I looked up and saw his height. I did a double-take when he arrived, as he was not just your average six feet! He had to duck to get through my doorway when he entered my tiny studio apartment; oh yes, he was six feet six inches tall! We were both a little uncomfortable. He had a special evening planned; we went to a movie then to dinner. Obviously, it was a memorable night, as it led us to the altar!

During their courtship, Grandma learned that Frank had been married once before, and his wife had died during childbirth along with his only child. It's hard to believe she was only twenty-five when she first met him, and he was forty-two. When I learned of their age difference, I asked myself, does age matter? Can a relationship with a seventeen-year age gap even survive? It seems today the odds are stacked against you, but their love was able to withstand the test of time. Learning of the loss of his wife and son had quite an impact on Dorothy. She realized the fragility of life, which made her appreciate every moment she had with her loved ones. She thought, "He had a little boy he will never know. Not to mention he had to forge on without his wife."

Frank was raised Catholic and was a handsome looking, six-foot-tall man, sporting a thick deep red head of hair with shiny silver sideburns. Despite their age difference, it was only a matter of time before he would sweep Dorothy off her feet. Grandma once described him as having wavy silver hair and clear blue eyes framed by his glasses. Dorothy was Lutheran, had blue eyes, fair skin, and a beautiful smile that won over many a heart. She had a warm, jovial laugh that was contagious and always brought a smile to Grandpa's face and countless others. She was a strong-willed, hard-working, practical German woman who dressed simply and yet always wore a freshly starched apron over her open button-up housedresses. Grandma insisted her clothes had to be freshly pressed, without a wrinkle. My mom used to enjoy ironing and found comfort in the process of pressing the family's clothes; this is not an attribute I at all inherited.

Their love continued to grow for each other as time matured. Grandpa liked surprising her by giving her small gifts, which were something she was not accustomed to and was often touched by his thoughtfulness. He had a way of wooing her not just with gifts but sweet love notes he left in unexpected places:

"Dorothy my love, each day I am with you I grow to love you so much more. Your will to pursue your dream inspires me to be a better man. You, my love, make me a better person. I loved you from the moment I met you and will never stop loving you." Frank

He saved first edition dimes, and each of them was placed in a collector's coin card. To show his ongoing love for her he wrote, "Your lover forever. -Frank." To him, those dimes represented moments of special events they shared with one another. By leaving love

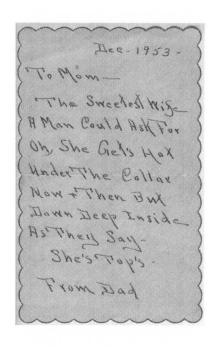

notes with first edition dimes around the house for Dorothy to find it seemed that Frank figured out a way to capture her heart forever with his kindness and always made her feel so special.

His gentle way of letting her know how much she meant to him melted her heart. Frank not only wrote something charming, but genuinely put thought into his writing. He had beautiful penmanship for a man. He wrote many of his sweet love letters addressing her as "Mom." I suppose it is because she was such a caring and giving mom, not just to my mother, but also to the many children who needed her.

I remember hearing my mom and grandma telling me he would continue to write her love letters throughout his life and leave them all over the house for her to find. Grandpa certainly knew how to capture her affection. The love notes Grandpa wrote were one of many desirable and sweet characteristics about him that stole Grandma's, heart. I don't know of a woman who wouldn't melt with notes and gestures like this. When I think about all the nuances of keeping the romance alive, my grandfather set great examples.

One thing is for sure; when it came to money, my grandmother was in charge. She had a goal, and she would not deviate to accomplish her dreams. Although Frank was an intense, heartfelt Irishman, he knew she was in control, as she was the levelheaded partner in the relationship. She somehow managed not to make him feel at any time less of a man, and when making decisions, she would allow him to feel as though his input was nonetheless valuable. I found this quality in her to be so admirable because it's so important to make a man, lover or partner feel valued, as opposed to the man bashing we so often see or hear about in our world today.

Grandpa blended well with Grandma's family, although they didn't want to see her agree with all his views, as she was looked upon as the matriarch of her family to ensure everyone was financially stable. Her family was not as giving as she was. He saw this and soon realized their selfish behavior and excessive greed. I suppose the Great Depression created financial anxiety, causing her family to worry that their wealth could be taken away from them without notice. She had a sense of obligation to her family, especially to her mother. Their caring ways was an amazing quality they shared, which made their love for one another so incredibly unique.

My grandparent's courtship up to their engagement was right out of a fairy tale, as she believed Frank was her knight in shining armor. As a little girl, I got my first glimpse of romance from "Cinderella." I fantasized about meeting a man who would rescue me, and we would live happily ever after. I think as young girls, we all at some point imagine our wedding. We all believe true love waits and marriage is 'til death do us part.' My ideas were just that: a princess looking for her prince.

For me, meeting my husband was very much unexpected. Going out on a blind date was something that never would have crossed my mind; in retrospect, I'm grateful I kept an open mind. Otherwise, my husband and I never would have met. Many doubts went through my head about a blind date working out, and honestly, I almost found myself sabotaging it. I certainly didn't plan to fall in love; it just sneaked up on me. In my case, it was sooner than later as his many gestures melted my heart, similarly to the way Grandpa did with Grandma!

When Grandpa picked her up for a date, he would always make sure he opened the car door for her. Those gentlemanly actions were something Grandpa never lost sight of and something today would warm the heart of most any woman. He took her to dinner, dancing, and walks through the park. To top off their awe-struck evenings, even though they lived in the same boarding house, he would make a point to walk her to the front door and give her a soft, gentle peck on the cheek. All the romantic signals that make a girl blush.

Right down to their engagement, Frank could not have planned a more special evening. He knew not to buy a lavish big diamond ring, as Grandma was a humble, and simple woman. Frank surprised her with what she thought was a normal date and turned the evening into an unforgettable proposal. He took her to her favorite restaurant. They sat at their usual booth, always sitting close to one another.

Like so many other nights, they strolled back to her apartment, and he gently grabbed her hand and spun her around. Much to her amazement, Frank got down on one knee with a tiny black box open with a touch of sparkle. The ring was modest but exquisite.

He looked up at her and asked, "I have known from the moment I met you I would spend the rest of my life with you. I can't imagine growing old without you in my life. Dorothy Burr, will you do me the honor and marry me?"

Surprised at Frank's gesture, a tear emerged from her eye along with a huge smile saying, "YES, YES, YES!"

My grandfather may have known from the moment he met my grandma, but at that instant, their magical true love seemed so unique. As I reflect back on my grandma's life, through the eyes of my mom, it reminds me of the kind of love they shared, where two souls connect to the end. As destiny would have it, Frank was the missing piece to her puzzle, and once she realized this, everything in her life made sense. Dorothy was the breath of his life that filled his heart with love and joy. I am grateful my husband and I have a deep connection to one another and a mutual respect towards each other.

In marriage, it is customary for the bride to take on the groom's last name; however, Frank felt Dorothy Burr's last name held more stature than his. Although today this is a more common practice, during that era it was unusual for the bride not to take the groom's last name. He expressed his feelings about this to her but she, of course, would have it no other way but to take on the Doyle name.

Her love for Grandpa would continue to flourish. He would often let her make major decisions to allow her visions to come alive, prosper and grow because he knew the many sacrifices she had made growing up to ensure a better life for her and her family. Self-sacrifice is the ultimate expression of love. We can all relate to the feeling of falling in love, the romance, and passion. We never want that sensation to go away.

The reality of what I instinctively knew but didn't want to admit—that the blissfully happy times of flowers and romance can quickly become a distant memory if taken for granted—is all too true. After twenty some odd years of marriage I understand that the honeymoon period fades. Almost all relationships have difficulties; what I have learned is to put your spouse first. Listening, showing patience, compassion, and forgiveness are the characteristics, that are critical in keeping a marriage alive. I admire my Grandma and Grandpa for keeping their love alive until my grandfather passed away in 1960. They were together for thirty-two years.

My beloved grandparents were united in marriage at the parsonage of St. Paul's Lutheran Church in Zelienople, Pennsylvania, on Thursday, December 20, 1928. They invited family and close friends to keep the wedding intimate and small. As with most traditional marriage ceremonies, the dress is the highlight for the bride. My grandma's sense of style was down-to-earth, and so was her dress. She wore beautiful baby's breath in her hair and carried a bouquet of red and white roses. Her dress was modest but elegant, like the style of Audrey Hepburn, an ivory knee-length ball gown, and capped sleeves with a high slit-like neckline that extended onto the shoulders with a satin tulle skirt. Frank wore a beautiful black suit with a gorgeous red tie accompanied with a red rose boutonniere.

Their honeymoon in the New England states was brief. They stayed at a picturesque cottage on a lake. Just like what she had in mind for her weekend retreats. Grandma continually blushed as she told me that for the first couple of days they left their cabin only to take strolls around the lake. Frank was excited to take her out so he could show off his lovely new bride with whom he had fallen so head over heels in love.

They had an epic love affair, and his love notes continued throughout their entire marriage. Even at bedtime, Frank always made a point to say how much he loved her. When they argued, he would profess his love aloud. I learned that even in times of disagreement, my grandfather would bellow out to my mom at night while the two of them were lying side-by-side, and Joni was in her bedroom, "Joni, tell your mother I love her." In turn, Grandma would say the same "Tell your daddy I love him too." This story reminds me of "The Walton's," where their mom and dad would start by saying goodnight to all their children, and in turn, their children would say goodnight one by one, making it take way too long to say goodnight. I love how my grandparents were so sweet to each other, as it reinforced the message of their devotion to one another.

My parents passed this down to me, and I must confess, I say goodnight every night to my family. As the bewitching hour approaches for bedtime with a flip of the light switch standing in the darkness, "Goodnight my dear children, I love you, sleep tight, and don't let the bedbugs bite!"

As they began their new life together, the newlyweds continued to live at the boarding house. She continued her work at the hospital and Frank with sales.

I guess it was about four years after my grandparents were married that they had saved enough money to complete the purchase of the land in the country. As Mom would proudly recant their story, Grandma's brothers, Bill and George would continue to help and collaborate where they would soon build the resort to be a place where families would return, year after year. Her long-awaited dream would soon be a reality. The land was a beautiful, charming sanctuary where she was to build cottages for a place to retreat to in the summer.

The largest cabin built on the grounds of Grandma's Wonderland Park

Grandpa would also contribute his time and efforts to making this long-awaited hideaway for people from all over to visit. In some ways, I feel this was my grandfather's way of showing my grandma's family how much he loved her and how he wanted her to achieve her dreams. Grandma wanted to make the cottages a home away from home, so she made sure each one had a warm and homey feel. The original cottages were built alongside Connoquenessing Creek, which is the town where St. John's Lutheran Church resides today and where my grandparents are buried side by side. Interestingly, Connoquenessing is an Indian word which means a long way straight, so I guess the creek must have been long and straight.

All the homes were furnished with cookware, and Grandma would go to the Goodwill and pick up any piece she thought might add to the ambiance of the cottages. Unfortunately, there were no modern-day bathrooms in the bungalows; however, each one did have an outhouse so on chilly nights this made for a brisk walk.

The vacationers didn't mind making this sacrifice of having to walk outside to use the bathroom in the cold as the resort was so beautiful.

Grandma realized that for many, the summer cottage was not only where one goes to get away from the hustle and bustle of the city but a quiet, home away from home in which they could organize their lives. More importantly, a place to reflect on their year, the good and the bad, so it was much more than just spending free time. She also hoped her cottages would attract repeat vacationers, and they would consider this countryside cottage a second home.

Mom fondly told my sister and me how much the farm meant to Grandma. She conveyed to Frank her thoughts on how special she wanted this place to be for their guests,

"Frank, when someone comes to get away and forget their worries, I want them to be able to lay their head on a pillow and sink into the comforts of familiar surroundings. Where each person can leave a mark left by their hand or their foot and can feel the love and joy you and I built for lasting memories to cherish for now and forever."

Her thoughts here were lovely. With all the hustle and bustle we face in our mundane everyday life, what better notion could there be than to be able to leave your troubles behind while vacationing?

My parents would also find a peaceful vacation spot for us to visit annually. It became a tradition for my family and me to go to Treasure Island, Florida, the same place, and the same time every year. You may be wondering why we chose the same destination every year. It had everything we looked for in a vacation; it made it so much fun and magical. For us, it was the sun, beach, pool, and the shuffleboard court. My favorite was

Ron analyzing the game of shuffleboard

when we all had a shuffleboard playoff! I can picture my dad's "shit eating grin" each time he would win! In the first few years, it was my family and a few friends, and over time, the number of families would grow whom we would meet along the way.

As part of cottage life, Grandma's love for flowers was, of course, an asset to each place as well as the surrounding grounds. She wanted to plant flowers that would bloom as early as spring and would continue to blossom throughout the summer. She planted lilacs, gardenias, lilies of the valley, and roses, which emitted an intense fragrance unique and yet complementing one another.

Tending to their gardens was just one of the many simple pleasures in life Grandma and Mom would crave every year. Sitting on the front porch was something Grandma cherished, and therefore, wanted to make this carefree pastime an experience for others to remember.

It was a place the whole family could enjoy and a relief for those to get away throughout the year, whether for a month, a week, or only a weekend; each day was a joy. It was meant and intentioned to leave all work and home stress behind! She wanted it to be an environment one could embark on where they could bring the comforts from their house to their home away from home. By bringing some of their familiar surroundings from homes such as their pets, or a bike to ride along the countryside, made it that much more special. She wanted people to find a place where one could rejuvenate with no hurries. Getting away from the hustle and bustle of one's everyday life, Dorothy strongly felt that this retreat that she created would be a luxury by just slowing down and smelling the flowers, taking long walks, fishing in the creek, and even picking fresh wild berries.

As more cottages were built, my grandparents rented them out on a weekly basis. These were exciting times for the two of them as the homes were always reserved. They advertised their rentals in the *Pittsburgh Press*. It wasn't long before the business was booming and they had a waiting list. As the resort's popularity grew, the rental properties quickly became more work than the family could handle, so they hired help to maintain the grounds, as well as to do the cleaning and to prepare the bungalows for the vacationers.

Soon the number of cottages went from fifteen to eighteen. People celebrated family reunions, and this would sometimes mean they would require using two or more of the houses. As the resort grew, my grandparents realized a dance hall would be an excellent place for vacationers to gather. They wanted it to show the charm of the Pennsylvania countryside, blending a distinctive old-fashioned character with a country dining ambiance, based on making their food and sharing it with others. It was a warm and inviting atmosphere to attract the whole family.

As little girls, my sister and I loved to visit the pavilion. We would imagine Grandma and Mom experiencing the music where vacationers would come to dance and socialize. To me it seemed nothing mattered when you entered the hall; it was so much fun to pretend we were dancing with our princes. It makes me giggle when I think of how girly-girl we both were!

The dance hall was built in the early 1900's. The decor featured a stone fireplace and beamed cathedral ceilings. The beautiful oak hardwood floor was destined over the years to show all the scuffs and dings formed by the happy feet that danced across it. In time, Grandpa built a spectacular waterfall just outside the dance hall with a gazebo surrounded by Grandma's flowers. A picnic area nestled in the woods was just a few feet away. On Saturday nights, the dance hall hosted bands, from jazz to country. Square dancing became a favorite with vacationers. It was evident the resort was a success.

Anyone who knew Joni knew she was not particularly shy. She was outspoken, and some of her stories shocked my sister and me. This story will forever go down in the history books as one of her best.

On occasion, my grandparents joined in on the fun and attended the festivities. One evening they sat side by side in the gazebo gazing at the stars, surrounded by the glow of fireflies. Frank caressed Dorothy's hair and whispered in her ear, "Let's make love under the stars."

I chuckled as I knew Grandma was old fashioned, and could not possibly imagine her doing such a thing out in the open; but apparently, I was wrong. Much to my surprise, she was a little vixen.

She expressed, "What better way to top off a perfect hot summer night than to get down to business under the stars!" "Frank, what if we get caught?" Dorothy whispered.

Frank began unbuttoning her dress, kissing her gently on the lips, inching his way to her breasts. "Dorothy, that's what makes it so much more fun, the thought of possibly getting caught!"

The idea of being naughty under the stars ignited Dorothy's lust for Frank. She could not resist and began to kiss him passionately. Both were so caught up in the moment they quickly forgot about all the people dancing the night away nearby in the dance hall. They weren't caught, and I was told that was a night never to be forgotten.

Chapter 3

Joni and Twenty-Eight Babies

It was the peak of the Depression, and everyone had to adjust to a different way of living; most of their friends lost their jobs and had to make do with little or nothing. During this time, people did what they had to do to make ends meet. When looking back on my grandparents and what they did, I think it was ingenious: they decided to rent a house in downtown Pittsburgh and help other families in need of daycare. Grandma still worked at the hospital, but she applied for a foster care license, as she wanted to help families. Obtaining a foster care license was not only a way of helping many children, but it provided a small subsidy on a monthly basis.

Fortunately, she was also a registered nurse and was able to find work quickly. She advertised her childcare services to several organizations such as St. Paul's Catholic Orphanage, the Bradley A. Center Home for Children, and Rosalie Foundling Home; her degree in nursing was extremely helpful in attracting clients to the daycare center.

I don't know how she did it, but between 1935 and 1939, Grandma cared for twenty-eight babies and toddlers. During those four years, mom was blessed to be one of these children.

Through Grandma's generosity and love for children, she made me recognize that every child matters and every life matters. Foster parents who take in a child can make all the difference in the world for generations to come by making them feel loved and not forgotten.

The house my grandparents rented had ten rooms; the first two floors accommodated all the children. They had several girls who helped with the children; their quarters were on the third floor. To this day I will never know how my grandmother took care of all those children; I had two, who are seven years apart, and I thought that was hard, but twenty-eight, all at once, and all close in age is unfathomable.

At Grandma's daycare, everyone had, a role in taking care of the children. There were approximately four others hired to help manage the daycare. One of Grandpa's responsibilities was providing transportation for everyone to get back and forth from their homes to the daycare house. Sometimes on their days off, Frank would drive them into the city to shop for groceries. He also drove Grandma to thrift stores, as she would search for the best bargains for both the resort and daycare.

Come to find out Grandpa was handy with a hammer. Making all the repairs in the house became his responsibility. He sometimes would help cook and clean, and prided himself on knowing his way around the kitchen. Times have since changed, but back then society saw women as the cooks; but I think it was so wonderful Grandpa wasn't afraid to slap on an apron and assemble a meal. Now that's an exceptional man considering it was the 1930s.

I recall my grandma planted a garden to help feed all those hungry mouths. She grew green beans, carrots, onions, radishes, tomatoes, lettuce, corn, and rhubarb. My mother also used to grow a large garden; I remember the love she had of harvesting her fresh vegetables. There would be times while she was cooking supper she would run out and pick fresh green beans, quickly snap them, cook them in a pot of water, and serve them up.

I was always so curious about the rhubarb she grew every year. As a young girl, I remember pulling a stalk right off the plant, taking a big bite and spitting it right out. Yuck! It was sour and made my mouth pucker. Mom grew a few strawberries, and she would add sugar along with the rhubarb, and make a pie. Mom's strawberry-rhubarb pie, it is one of my favorite childhood memories. To this day, it still makes me feel warm and fuzzy when I think of sitting at her table and eating warm strawberry-rhubarb pie.

By the sounds of it, an incredible amount of work went into taking care of all the children. Listening to her recount the story of the wringer washer was a reality check for me, as I did not have to endure such manual labor when washing clothes. Apparently, it was always going; there were no disposable diapers, and each bottle needed sterilizing on a bottle rack in boiling water. Washing machines have come a long way since the 1930s. In today's world, we all use automatic washing machines. We only throw our clothes in the tub along with soap, close the lid, turn the dial to your desired setting and wait for forty to fifty minutes, and voila, you have clean clothes.

The wringer washer, however, required you scrub your clothes out by hand. It makes me tired just thinking about it. Can you imagine how time-consuming it must have been to clean twenty-eight children's clothes and diapers? Once all the garments went through the wash, they were hung outside on the clothesline to dry in the summer months. In the basement, there were several clotheslines to hang the clothes to dry in the winter. Of course, they were always full. I could never forget my mother hanging our linens outside, and our clothes always smelled so fresh from the crisp air, dried by the sun and the warm breeze; I miss those days.

The children they cared for came from all social classes. There was one little girl named Ruthie who came to Grandma when she was just eight weeks old. Her father was a wealthy Italian man named Joe who owned a used car dealership in Altoona, Pennsylvania. He was tall with thick black hair and dark bronzed skin. He had dashing brown eyes, which displayed a sense of maturity and confidence along with an easy smile. As with Italian men, he had a reputation for charming women, and he didn't have to rely on his looks alone. He had it all: he was sultry, suave, and according to Grandma, he knew how to flirt with the women.

Ruthie's mother was a young girl who immigrated to the United States from Ireland; she and Joe fell in love, her family was furious. Her parents did not give permission for her to marry him; during that era, it was frowned upon for an Italian boy to bring home an Irish girl, and vice-versa. Ruthie's mother couldn't afford to care for her, and she was far too young, so as heartbreaking as it was for her, she had no choice but to give Joe full custody.

Due to Joe's work schedule, he needed to find a reliable resource to care for his daughter. After researching his options, Grandma and her reliable services were highly recommended by several people. Being a man of good fortune, he could pay quite well for Ruthie's care; there were times he even paid in advance. Ruthie had only the best money could buy, and she would often share her clothes with some of the other little girls. My mother was fortunate that she was one of those little girls.

As Mom continued to live amongst the other children the Doyle's had taken in, she saw many of the children come and go.

Ruthie, on the other hand, stayed long after the others left. She felt so lucky to have Ruthie as her friend. One-day Mom received an invitation to a birthday party. She was so happy to get the invitation, but not sure if she wanted to go as she had nothing to wear.

"What's the matter with you, I thought you would be overjoyed getting to go to your first party?"

She looked up with a frown on her face and replied, wiping her wet cheeks, "Nothing, I don't have anything cute or pretty to wear so I can't go to this party."

All Joni could think about was how delightful a birthday party with a cake, singing, and games would be. They sure are a big deal to little kids. Even though Mom was not the birthday girl, she wanted to dress appropriately, like a princess. Ruthie graciously came to the rescue; she offered Mom to choose from several dresses she had.

Joni was precious to the Doyles; although they could not afford to buy a lovely outfit for her, Grandma was blessed Ruthie had a beautiful dress to share with her. From what mom recalled of the little blue dress, it was similar to what Cinderella wore; it was so lovely with layers of chiffon that flowed when she twirled. There was a tiny bit of beading on the bodice, which emphasized the sweetheart neckline and she said it fit her perfectly.

Joni arrived at the party looking and feeling beautiful in her blue dress. Not a bit different than today, when she walked in, kids were screaming, running through the house with floating balloons drifting aimlessly, and a stack of unopened presents on a table nearby the cake. Joni was so proud of the gift she got for the birthday girl; she hurriedly placed it amongst all the other gifts. She helped Grandma wrap the present with a red silk bow tied neatly around it. In the box was a doll with long brunette hair wearing a pink dress.

The cake was huge and covered in thick chocolate icing—even decorated with tiny pink flowers to match the decor. Streamers and banners covered the room. Mom smiled so big as she continued recounting with such detail. She referred to all the kids having party hats, and even their dog was wearing one of those pint-sized pointy hats. Mom recalled having quite the sweet tooth and couldn't wait to sing Happy Birthday so she could get a piece of cake. What a beautiful day and great first party it was for her.

When the weather was pleasant, Grandma would encourage Mom and the others to go outside. Most of the kids used to run around barefoot typically wearing a pair of shorts and a plain t-shirt. There was no designer fashion active wear for the kids during this time, as nobody could afford them, least of all the middle-class families. When it sprinkled, the kids wanted to be in the open air. Pitter-patter, pitter-patter as the rain fell against the window.

"I want to go out and play, Mother," Joni lamented. "When will it stop?"

Grandma, of course, wanted the rain to end as well, as she too wanted the children to be able to go outdoors.

"I'm sure it will stop soon. In the meantime, why don't you all come and gather around to help me put together a puzzle."

Apparently, Joni was not at all interested and ran into the living room, threw herself on the floor, and sighed. "I just want to play in the rain."

Grandma thought to herself, "It's not coming down too terribly bad, and it's a hot summer day, after all, why not?" She decided it was a good way for the children to burn off some energy. "All right, I suppose there is no reason you all can't play in the yard, how many of you would like that?"

With that, many of the children who were bored, including Joni, smiled, and began jumping all around, "me, me too, I want to go!"

Puddles were all over the backyard, streets, and side-walks. As the kids began to run towards the door, none of them were concerned about putting on their jackets or boots. After all, it was sweltering hot, why bother. The cloudburst was bursting with rain all around them, soaking their clothes. They all began laughing and hopping in the wet puddles. Water was everywhere, and the kids were so excited to be dashing about and splashing.

Grandma watched from the porch; she asked Joni and the others, "Are you having fun?"

They did not want to come in the house; they were having too much fun. They scurried around in circles

Joni showing off her hula moves

waving their arms in the air as they tried to catch the raindrops in their mouths. Mom even remembered the birds taking cover in the trees as they watched them race to snatch a worm out of the wet grass. That night, when it was time for Joni to go to bed, she thought how glad she was for the liquid sunshine and how much fun she and the others had together.

Through the years, Joni continued to thrive under the couple's care. Though it's difficult to think of, Mom was the only child in the Doyles that had no contact with their biological parents. Thank God, for the goodness and kindness of Frank and Dorothy, she didn't know any different. At times, Joni was a bit confused since the other kids would come and go, as they should, while Joni continued to stay in the house. Despite the insecurities my mom was feeling, she always felt love and joy from the Doyle's. Mom did say, however, that while growing up, there was always a fear in the back of her head of her birth mother coming for her.

I think Grandma believed Iva had good intentions of coming back, but she never did. I later found out the story she told my grandparents was not right. She told them my mom was illegitimate and she did not have any money. The fact that my mom was born out of wedlock is correct. I do know when Iva found out she was pregnant with my mom she hid it from her family as long as she could.

I later learned Iva was married to a man she never had children with and his last name was Johnson. Apparently, he was in the service and was gone most of the time. They didn't see each other much at all due to him traveling all over the world while enlisted in the military. They never divorced one another, but she continued to carry his last name. She lived a somewhat comfortable life supported by his life in the military. None of us knows much about her involvement with Jack Goulding . . . her lover. It was our understanding that the other children by him, Jerry and Jack, and twins Jim and Joyce were Mom's biological siblings. To my knowledge, Iva was a successful district manager for Avon and traveled a lot. Apparently, this is how she might have met Jack.

Until Mom could retrieve her birth certificate, she did not know how her name read on it. Once found, she saw that the

Goulding name was on it. It read, Joan Goulding. She never met him, and it was never really confirmed he truly was her biological father. I believe he was since the birth certificate confirmed "Goulding" as her last name. In the meantime, Frank and Dorothy implored a woman who worked in the legal aid department to help them find out more about Mom's birth parents. Mom could not imagine anyone else being her mother just because they shared DNA. Dorothy was the mother she loved and the only mother she ever knew.

With the understanding of the legal measures to consider in attempting the adoption process, they forged forward to find Iva. My grandparents were able to determine Iva was thirty-eight years old when she gave birth to Mom. My great-grandparents had helped Iva support and raise her other children. The day she handed my mother over on a street corner to the Doyle's, my grandma believed it would only be temporary.

Joni made up a story that she moved in with the Doyle's because, in her mind, she felt they needed her to be happy. Her birth parents were somewhat a mystery. It seemed okay to make up this little white lie as she felt it was the truth. She once told her kindergarten teacher she packed a suitcase, and they came for her; this is how she came to live with them. Joni believed if she misbehaved, the Doyle's would send her away. Little did my mom know how much they truly adored her. I sometimes wonder how she could have missed this, given my grandparent's love.

On the other hand, Dorothy's family did not much care for my mom because she did not share their German bloodline. There was a time when Mae, Dorothy's mother, wanted her to give my mom up for adoption. Interestingly, it was not something my grandma could have done, as Iva did not relinquish those rights.

My mom overheard a conversation Grandma had with Mae,

"You need to either get in touch with this Iva or find out if she is going to come back for Joni or you have no choice but to give her up for adoption."

Still rattled, Grandma replied, "I have no intention whatsoever of sending her away, she desperately needs us, and quite frankly, I need her. I love her as if she were my daughter. Despite Iva's troubled past, I am convinced she picked me for a reason and I am a good mother to Joni!"

Mae stumbled towards Dorothy and pointed with her finger, "Well how is it going to appear with you bringing up this child as she looks nothing like us?"

The Burr's, Dorothy's side of the family, were short with a fair complexion and light-colored eyes. As for Joni, she was much taller, thin, wavy jet-black hair, black eyes, and deep olive skin. It makes me so irritated to think of how traumatic this must have been for my mom to overhear. What can be more agonizing for a young child to be stunned with that kind of information as to whether she belonged to the woman she called Mom?

Mae winced, "You don't even really know her ethnicity, and it's evident just by looking at her skin she is not German. How will you ever know what her inherited traits might be?"

Grandma burst into tears as she wiped her face, "Joan is a gift from God, and I love her like my own."

"What are you going to do if Iva should come back for her?" Mae responded.

Grandma was mad as a wet hen, her shoulders shook with angry sobs, "I will be heartbroken, but I don't think it is ever going to happen, as she has not made any attempts to come back for her! Besides she knows she is well taken care of and most of all, loved!"

Grandma turned away, her nose and cheeks were red from crying, "Enough, I don't ever want to hear another word of you considering adoption for Joni!"

There was silence, as I think Mae was in shock Grandma shut her down. She picked up her things and instantly left. "Fine you will never hear me speak another word, but just know, I don't agree with your decisions!"

I sometimes think about this and can't fathom the horror Grandma and Mom experienced at that moment. I know, as a child grows up, family and friends are quick to point out how children look like their mother or father. From my mom's eyes, at an early age, Joni knew she looked nothing like the Burrs. Luckily, Mom always knew the Doyles took her in, and Grandma never kept it a secret. Joni was Frank and Dorothy's child; after all, they were raising her. They brought her up with the same traditions, and most importantly, she was loved.

At a young age, mom's cousins let her know that there was no question she was not blood. I was never sure how Mom really felt about this, but it never stopped the Doyle's from loving her. She knew growing up they were not her birth parents, but it was not a big deal to her. She didn't spend much time wondering who they were, nor the reasons she ended up where she did.

It infuriates me to know the relatives were never discreet with their comments; and when the family gathered for family picnics and such, Joni would overhear others ask Grandma if she was going to keep her. She knew she did not look like any of them, but she also knew Dorothy and Frank did not intend to give her up. Both were affectionate and would cuddle her in the folds of their arms along with the simple words spoken aloud daily, "I love you." To this day, I don't think the Burrs realized the profound love my mom and grandmother shared with each other.

Grandma would never allow Iva to march in and just snatch her away as my grandparents were all she knew as her parents. I have to believe if Iva had come back for my mom, Grandma would have fought with her life to keep her. I'm not sure why my grandparents did not have children of their own. I believe my grandparents had such fulfilling lives taking care of everybody else's children it must not have been a priority. They never lost sight of letting Joni know she was special and beautiful. As the years passed, she began to feel so fortunate knowing they would always make her feel protected and safe. She also felt lucky as she realized she could have easily gotten lost in the system and would have become an orphan.

One-day Grandma explained to Mom the best she could how she arrived and why she remained in her care. It was if a ton of bricks had been lifted off her shoulders because she felt Mom deserved to know the truth. She then enrolled her in the local school system. To her surprise, it was easier than she could have imagined. After all, she didn't have any adoption papers in place. Grandma just stated the truth: She was her foster mother, and her given name was Joan Helen Goulding Doyle. Doyle was special to her because she and Frank wanted her to have their last name. It was never made legal in the sense of adoption, but Grandma did it anyway.

Over the years growing up, I would hear increasingly from my mom about her childhood. The stories she shared were fascinating to me. I wanted to know more, always more to be a part of her life.

Grandma took Mom shopping whenever she could afford to buy her nice clothes. On one particular occasion, Mom fondly remembered Grandma buying her a beautiful white dress. Although Dorothy was frugal, Grandma would get nothing but the finest for her baby. I think this was her way of showing my mother she belonged with them. Joni got new patent leather shoes and a white ribbon for her hair. She felt like a princess when both her mother and father walked her to the front of the church to be baptized at the little Lutheran church.

This particular church was where Joni received her baptism, and Dorothy's great-grandfather founded this church; where her family had roots in this community. Her parents were buried there, along with the entire Burr family. Being the thoughtful individuals they were, my grandparents purchased plots for themselves, long before their time. To this day, Frank's Irish name is reminiscent, as Dorothy lies right beside him announcing to all her love for him and her faith in God.

They may have been of different religious backgrounds, but they respected each other's beliefs and believed in one God and Savior. I know this from the values they placed in faith and how they raised her as well as me. I remember my mom recounting a fond memory of watching her father make the sign of the cross each night after he said his prayers with her, before tucking her safely in bed.

Being baptized was a formal document acknowledging Joni's existence and the fact that the Doyle's were her legal guardians. It was that piece of paper Grandma brought to the school to prove that she and Frank were responsible for her. It is the day that she was accepted and welcomed into their entire family, and of course, she was overwhelmed with joy. She now knew she would never have to face being taken away; it was then she felt they were her actual parents.

I do know the insecurities my mom felt by not being legally adopted, but according to her, my grandparents did not give up on the idea to make it official either. Their next move was to make a trip to Harrisburg, where she was born, to visit the courts in hopes to secure her adoption. My grandparents, of course, knew her birth mother's name was Iva, and she had four other siblings. They never knew for sure who her biological father was; however, it didn't much matter.

I know very little about Mom's biological father. To my knowledge, my great-grandparents were English, Irish, and German on Iva's side. Mom mentioned my great-grandfather's name was Benjamin and great-grandmother's name was Emma. Grandma told my mom her biological father was Jewish and married; his name was Mr. Goulding and that he took Iva as his mistress. Apparently, Iva's parents were very much involved in her other four children. It was weird to think my mom had four other siblings and I had aunts and uncles I never really knew.

As I recall Mom's grandfather once told her she was much better off where she ended up, and it was a blessing to be with the Doyle's. In later years, she would learn this to be true as she discovered they had a difficult upbringing. Mom told me my great-grandfather established a trucking firm and this is how he made his living. Iva also had two brothers, whom my mother never met. It was apparent Iva was a challenge to my great-grandfather.

Shortly after Iva gave birth to my mom, she fell into a deep depression and required much more care than her family could provide, and eventually ended up in a sanitarium that accepted women following pregnancy. In the 1930s, doctors knew very little about postpartum depression (PPD). My great-grandparents became the full-time caregivers for Iva's other children. It is evident why they pressured Iva to give up my mother; they, in no way, had the physical or emotional capacity to care for another child. I have often wondered if her depression emerged from giving up Mom. The reality of the situation is, from the time Iva found out she was pregnant with Joni, she feared the negative response her parents would display, and rightfully so.

Becoming a new parent is never a cakewalk, but adding such a debilitating condition such as postpartum depression on top of being a single mom of four would be more than anyone could handle. As a layperson, I don't completely understand all the circumstances involved with PPD. There have been numerous times I wondered how some women would experience this mentally, and often debilitating, condition, to different degrees for different lengths of time and other women have no problems at all. With the advancement of modern medicine, and studies addressing this issue, for women who now receive the diagnosis of PPD there is hope, appropriate treatment, and support.

In Mother's generation, there was not only a lack of understanding in the medical and mental health professions but also just common knowledge in general; essentially, there was no support. In Iva's situation, even though she tried to hide her pregnancy, it was obvious people would soon find out. I have no doubt in my mind, knowing the reality that she had to give up my mom while she was still carrying her had to be emotionally heartbreaking; I am sure this added to her depression and created an enormous amount of anxiety for her. It makes me so sad just thinking about the possibility of having to give up a child; I know Iva must have been overwhelmed with emotions.

Grandma finally located a lawyer in Harrisburg, Pennsylvania, who did much research on Iva. The license plate number Frank had written down the day they first met her was the key to their ability to obtain this information. Most people who are given up at birth, yearn to one day find their birth mother. However, in Joni's case locating her biological parents was the furthest thing from her mind. The people, who became family to her, and the sometimes-shocking twists and turns in her life, led her to understand what she finally came to realize: She was blessed to be unwanted.

Chapter 4

Joni's Childhood Memories

I remember the stories my mother shared with me explaining her reservations about the "Rag Man." I suspect fear and skepticism developed in her mind because children would come and go so much. According to my mom, he would stroll down the street once a week with an old gray mare pulling his rickety old wagon. He would call out in a deep, loud voice, "Rags, any rags today?" as he would slowly make his way down the pavement.

Whenever Mom heard him, no matter what was happening, she would make a beeline and hide under her parent's bed; Mom was sure he was the one responsible for the children disappearing one by one. At the time, she did not understand why the other kids would come and go as they did. My mom remained unseen under the bed until "Rag Man's" voice faded completely out. It was unfortunate; I think she was just afraid of the way he looked and sounded.

Mother continued with her story, which I found to be so fascinating that she was one of the twenty-eight children that Frank and Dorothy watched over. She was only nine years old in 1945 while struggling through the Depression. As with most Americans during this time they had to budget to make ends meet.

They worked hard, did without, and saved every penny they could. She frequently would accompany her mother to the grocery store and saw her use ration stamps. It is so crazy to think the Government found it necessary to ration food, gas, and even clothing during World War II. The Rationing Programs was put into place in 1942 and continued through 1946.

On one of their many trips to get canned foods at the local grocer, they would go to a nearby farm to buy eggs and chickens. They ate a lot of chicken, more than any other meat. According to my mom, it was due to the cost, as a chicken was more affordable than beef. I am surprised Mom still ate poultry after watching Grandma cut off a chicken's head! Grandma would kill them by severing their necks with an axe and then dunk it into scalding water to remove the feathers. After she plucked them and cleaned out the insides, she would place them in a bag to get them ready for frying. Recounting her story on several different occasions was certainly a reminder to my sister and me how lucky we were that we did not have to live through such hard times. I suppose you do what you have to do to survive, just not so sure I could have performed this act or for that matter, witness the beheading.

There was a big shade tree near the coop and a large stump under the tree with an axe planted in the middle. Grandma would catch the squawking victim with her hands and swiftly place the bird on the stump, holding it with one hand so that she had one free hand to grab the axe. With one swift blow, she would hurl the axe in the air and, POW

. . . just like that, she would part the head from the body.

Mom chuckled as she watched me squirm while telling me— she said, "The decapitated chicken would bounce, stagger, and run around without a head. It seemed like an eternity to my mom until the body would finally fall motionless to the ground."

Frank Doyle sporting his Pinkerton uniform

As disturbing as it was to watch, she somehow always managed to eat those chickens. I have to remember though, that for her family, it was a real treat to have a freshly fried hen for Sunday dinner. It became a family tradition to eat fried chicken every Sunday.

At the time, Grandpa was working at Pinkerton's as a security guard. It was a private agency established in the United States by Allan Pinkerton in 1850. Currently, it is a subsidiary of Securitas AB. He traveled to all the surrounding areas, delivering money to banks. As a young girl, Mom remembered the gun strapped to his hip. Grandpa used to wear it in the house, and she was often in awe of her daddy sporting a pistol on his waist. The idea of him carrying a gun while he worked made her wonder about the danger he might encounter.

She would look at his firearm and slowly raise her head to gaze into his eyes, "Are you a police officer; do you have to kill bad people?"

Grandpa was sitting on the couch after a long day at work, "Hey, come over, and sit next to your daddy."

She cautiously made her way next to her father, as she was unsure of his gun.

"No, I am not a police officer. The gun is primarily used to protect my partner and me when we deliver the money."

Mom thought he could have pulled the gun out at any time, but he didn't, as he was careful to lock it in a safe place. Thus, she was never made aware of its whereabouts.

"Oh, so you are not a police officer, I thought you had to be a police officer to carry a gun."

Frank, concerned about Joni's perception, realized he needed to reassure his reason for having the firearm.

"Well, I went through specialized training to prepare myself on how to use this weapon. Thank goodness I have never had to use it and hope I never will...but you just never know because there are some sick people out there that might try to steal the bags of money we transport."

She nestled in closer, and her dad wrapped his arms around her making her feel protected, "Daddy, you always make me feel safe . . . I love you."

Frank responded, "I love you, too Jiggy!" She earned that pet name, as whenever Frank would sing, she would dance the Irish Jig for him.

In the meantime, my grandparents faced a hard decision. Their landlord, Tom, who owned the rental property where they managed their daycare, decided they could no longer use the house as a center due to liability issues. It was shocking to them as they were helping so many families through these difficult times, and they felt blessed that Tom was an understanding landlord.

It was a long drive, and it was late when we arrived at my mom's house in Prescott, Arizona. We arrived late that night just a little before midnight, so we were tired. She had our beds all ready for us to fall into a slumber. The next morning when I was eating breakfast, my whole family, including my mom, was sitting at the kitchen table when she began telling us about the unfortunate time when my grandparents had to shut down their daycare.

Mom recalled, there was a sudden loud tapping at the door, Grandpa Frank said, "Don't bother; I'll answer it as it is probably somebody selling something, I'll just tell them nicely to go away." He opened the door thinking it was a salesman and it was Tom, their landlord.

"Oh, hey Tom, what do I owe the pleasure of you stopping over, I assumed it a salesperson at the door."

Tom's face was stone cold, with absolutely no expression. "I have some bad news for you and Dorothy; you have to shut down the daycare service."

"What, why?"

"It has been brought to my attention since you do not carry insurance for the house as a daycare center, I cannot allow you to continue to run it. I am sorry; I wish I had better news to deliver."

Dorothy overheard the conversation and quickly ran to the front door, "Tom you can't close the daycare!"

"You have to know I don't want to do this but I have no other choice. You must notify the children's parents immediately to let them know. I can give you a couple of weeks to help with the transition, but that is all I can do."

Dorothy was trying to hold back her tears, but once the first tear broke a stream of tears followed. Tom felt extremely sorry for Frank and Dorothy, "I wish I had better news to tell you, but this is out of my control as my hands are tied." Grandmother wiped her face; Frank hugged her and did his best to reassure her everything would be all right. "We will be ok." Frank tried to reassure her.

"Oh, Frank," she sobbed, "I am worried about the children, what will happen to them?" Frank could feel her heart breaking as she clung to him.

The next couple of weeks were tough on them, as they not only had to tell the parents but the help as well. Not sure how long they thought they could keep the daycare alive, I admire my grandparents for their commitment to caring for others during the Great Depression.

For every bad experience, every time of struggle, I can hear those words, "Everything happens for a reason!" I used to hate hearing those words, and my first thoughts were, "WHY, why me!" My parents, as well as my mentors in life, told me during tough times, "As difficult as it may be, there is always a blessing in it." At my most challenging times, I just couldn't see it; however, regarding pain, I do believe that time has a way of healing our wounded hearts. As for my grandparents, while they were experiencing a challenging point in their life, they could gain some wisdom and allow the next newfound adventure to emerge. They decided to take on another quest and seek to buy a house they could call their own.

Through determination and a lot of hard work, they eventually managed to save enough money to purchase the house Mom would grow up in on 514 Neville Street, in Pittsburgh,

Second house on the right is 514 N. Neville St., Pittsburgh PA

Pennsylvania. They knew what boarding house living was all about as they'd met each other in a rooming house. I suppose that is why they bought this vastly large house on Neville, as they saw the potential of renting out the rooms along with helping others. They did just that, rented all seventeen rooms. Each floor had several private rooms with a bathroom for the tenants to share.

Although the house on Craig Street was big, this home was gigantic to Mom. She often played hide and seek in the empty rooms. She used to beg her daddy to play with her. Often, Frank was too busy, but if he had work around the house, he would take some time and holler, "Joni, I am going to count to one hundred and close my eyes. Run and hide!"

Joni would quietly find a place where she knew her dad would not find her, "Daddy you will never find me now."

As he counted down, "97, 98, 99, 100 . . . OK, here I come, look out, look out wherever you are, I'm going to find you."

Joni would be as still as a mouse not moving a muscle if she could hear her daddy getting closer to her secret hiding spot; she would crawl and slither into a place where she was sure to fool him. They used to set limits on how long he would look for her, and if he couldn't find her in a ten-minute period, he would have to concede, "Olly, Olly oxen free, come out, come out wherever you are!"

That way she knew it was safe to come out and she would typically win. Mom was good at playing this game and being in a big house, she found all kinds of good hiding places and always kept it a secret.

Grandma and Grandpa intended to rent the rooms out on the main and second floor; Grandpa decided they would settle in the basement. In what little spare time Grandpa had, he partitioned rooms off as best he could. I can remember visiting as a young girl; they used clotheslines with blankets to divide the rooms. He managed to build a separate bedroom for himself and Grandma, as well as for Mom. Not having to share a bedroom any longer meant the world to her, since she always had to share a room with some of the other children in the house on Craig Street. Joni felt as though she always shared a room with someone who was messy. Their clutter became hers to clean up, as they would leave and she would be stuck cleaning it up.

It was such a pleasure that Grandpa made sure there was a workable bathroom for them to use and they would no longer have to share one with anyone else. I'm impressed with how skilled he was because he also built a functional kitchen where Dorothy cooked and later taught my mom how to prepare food. A rule that her parents enforced was never to wander in other parts of the house outside of the basement, especially when they began signing on tenants.

Once they finally got the house ready for occupants, their first tenant was Jimmy; Frank knew him, and he expressed interest in renting a room. He picked one of the smaller accommodations on the third floor. For single men and women wishing to live in a low-income space, boarding houses can be adequate housing, and for Jimmy, it was just what he needed.

Jimmy smoked, and that bothered Grandma; she said his room always smelled of cigarettes, and the wooden nightstand had cigarette burns all over it. It's a wonder he didn't burn the house down. Jimmy had very few clothes in his closet. It seemed as though he wore the same cardigan sweater with blue pants and a dark, thick jacket all the time. Jimmy was mostly bald with just a hint of gray around his temples; his gold-rimmed glasses were always on the verge of falling off the end of his nose. To my mom, he always looked like he needed a shave, and apparently he was missing a few teeth. There wasn't much conversation with anyone in the house; Mom thought perhaps this was because Jimmy was a cab driver and he talked to people all day and was tired of talking by the time he got home.

Mom's very first ride in a cab was with none other than Jimmy. She had always taken the streetcar in the winter and walked when the weather permitted. On days when he would take her in his cab, she felt so special, as it was a treat rather than walking in the harsh elements.

She felt sorry for Jimmy because, just like Mom, he had no relatives, so the Doyle's became his family. Mom soon discovered he had a fondness for alcohol; he tried his best to be discreet around her, but she could smell it on him.

On one occasion, Jimmy was acting quite peculiar, extra

jovial, and slurred his words a bit. He was always incredibly kind to Mom, and from time to time, he'd toss her a quarter and told her to save it for something nice. On one day, Jimmy threw Mom a silver dollar, and this was the first time she had seen one.

"Whoa, what is this? It sure is bigger than a quarter! Holy Cow! How much is this worth?" Joni was gushing over the coin.

Slurring his words, "Why Joan, it's a silver dollar and worth one whole dollar. I bet you can buy a whole lot of gumballs with that." Jimmy then turned and stumbled as he mumbled the words, "You're a good kid, now don't overeat on candy."

Then he staggered up the stairs to his room. Even though he acted a bit different than usual, Joni was grateful for a quarter as it meant a lot to her, but a dollar, well words couldn't begin to describe how she felt at the time. Her favorite candy was dark chocolate of any kind. She loved her chocolate, and there was no chance of her sharing.

Boarders Who Influenced Joni

I always enjoyed listening to Mom's childhood memories; they were always so fascinating. In my mind's eye, I can still hear the enthusiasm in her voice when she described the many boarders who came and went in her life. It amazed me at how she could recall so many of her fondest memories, as she would describe her encounters with some of the tenants. One of the things that I was always intrigued by with my mom is how she grew up in such a diverse environment with so many different kinds of people and personalities. As time went on, before she knew it, the house would soon fill up with all types of characters.

Bee became their next tenant. Bee was an incredible individual to Mom because she was so sweet to her. She kept to herself but always graced the house with a smile. Bee was a housekeeper for the Heinz family, of the Ketchup dynasty. These days, Heinz Ketchup is a staple found in most households across the world. Their estate was four blocks from their house on Neville.

The weather conditions never mattered, Bee typically walked to the mansion; however, from time to time Jimmy would give her rides in his cab if he was nearby. She worked long hours every day of the week except Sunday. Mom was very curious about the Heinz estate. It was just a few blocks away; the house was tucked behind huge trees and had a mysterious ambiance. Walking past the huge gray stone property, Mom and her friends were curious and dreamed of going inside. The house with its surrounding grounds comprised an entire street block in Shadyside, guarded by a six-foot-high black wrought iron fence. Tall bushes alongside the gates prevented any view of the grounds. At the driveway were massive entrance gates with a guard shack.

Mom said this was the only place you could sneak a glimpse of the estate; she was in complete astonishment Bee was able to go into that mysterious mansion each day. She said keeping everything clean for the Heinz family was important, as she was always picking up around their boarding house. She used to hum and sing, "Get a Job" by The Silhouettes as she cleaned. It was only a matter of time before Mom would soon hum along when she would tidy up. One day, Joni asked why she always hummed, "Joan, humming while you work is a soothing form of sound medicine. I don't need anyone telling me to get a job. I always had the sensibility that an honest day at work makes for healthy living."

Mom said Bee was not married; it's not that she didn't want too, but since she was working and making her own money, she chose to remain single. Mom didn't understand why Bee was so fond of that song, but now it makes sense, it reminded her every day she did not need a man to take care of her. It was not a secret where Bee worked, but she would never say exactly what her duties were, nor she would say anything about the Heinz family. Mom once asked Bee what she did in the mansion all day, and she was tight-lipped and maintained the family's privacy.

Bee's room was on the same floor as Jimmy's; they were friendly with one another. Jimmy always lit up like a Christmas tree when he saw her. In turn, she would get giddy around him when he complimented her. No matter what she wore, Jimmy told her how lovely she looked, even when she was wearing her uniform for work. Mom thought somehow that they would fall in love. Everybody deserves happiness in their life, and as they were alone, Mom had hopes of a fairytale ending for the two of them, they were so kind to her, but that fairy tale never happened.

Bee had chestnut brown hair that she wore pulled back in a knot with a dark, old-fashioned wave on the left side of her forehead; her clothes were very plain outside of her usual black and white uniform; she wore mainly dark brownish colors. Bright colors and patterns were not colors you would ever see her wear. According to my mother, it was apparent she did not care about brands or colors of clothes. Bee thought it was fashionable to wear a hairnet, as it kept every little hair on her head in place. Along with her boring outfit, she wore thick stockings with a distinct seam in the back of her legs. Mom recognized that Bee put them on with much care, as the seam was straight as an arrow. Whether she was coming or going, Bee always carried a small shopping bag that always looked full; full of what was unknown to Mom.

One day Mom eavesdropped on a conversation Bee was having with Jimmy on the front porch. Being a taxi driver, he had many exciting stories. Pittsburgh was a place where people from all over came to visit. He used to pick up many different people, and it seems that in his profession it wasn't unusual to get an earful whether he wanted to or not. There was always your average run of the mill, quiet person, but on occasion, he would hear some strange conversations, as well as witness crazy happenings in his rear-view mirror.

Some of the best times were when Mom would describe the people who lived in her house on Neville. She had a gleam in her eyes, and I immediately knew she was about to share another fabulous story about the people who lived there. I sat on the couch with my back pressed against the cushions and the sun pouring in through the same artful glass displayed at Grandma's house; she would share another scandalous story with me.

Apparently, Jimmy picked up a distinguished well-dressed gentleman on the East end of Shadyside. He requested Jimmy to get a woman a few blocks from where he lived. He also instructed, upon his arrival to honk twice. Beep, beep he pressed the horn. A gorgeous woman dressed in a stunning red dress wearing fishnet pantyhose, accessorized with black patent high-heeled shoes suddenly appeared on the curb.

Her hair color was a unique reddish mahogany, and she was fearlessly rocking red lipstick. I mean, not just your average red lips . . . bold RED! She looked fabulous! I think if she was to kiss anyone, and in this case, the distinguished man, she intended to leave her mark. The truth is, it sounded as though he enjoyed a little of her red lips on his body.

The man got out of the car and opened the door. Jimmy was awestruck by the woman's beauty. There was silence in the car, and then Jimmy said, "Where to?" The man said, "Just drive and keep the meter running." There were no words spoken in the back of the car, only the sound of lust, and a glimpse from his rear-view window. Jimmy drove them around the city for nearly an hour. My mom often wondered if the gentleman was married or someone famous; she even thought he could have been a politician.

I can imagine the look on Bee's face. Being the proper, prudent lady, she did not date for the sake of just dating. It sounds like she had very high standards and no man was good enough for her. Maybe that is why she was single, as she had such lofty expectations. Deep down I think she wished she were the mysterious woman in the back of that taxicab.

Bee lived at the boarding house for approximately eight years. As with most everyone who lived in the house, one of her favorite pastimes was sitting on the front porch. The purple morning glory vines that Grandma grew covered the porch from the railings up to the ceilings. How pretty they were, as she would say, "Dorothy has such a way with flowers, unlike me, her flowers are so lovely, and they make the porch being that much more inviting." She thought to herself; it was a place to sit, a place to relax, a place to pause. What a nice way to put it, as it was a remarkable place to ponder and smell the fresh air.

Mom had hoped that Bee would meet the man of her dreams, but I guess it wasn't meant to be. When she finally left, Mom often wondered if she moved into the Heinz estate, as she was such a loyal employee. She didn't know why she left but one thing was sure, everyone missed Bee a whole lot.

I often wonder why Bee moved on. I guess we will never know! Upon her departure, her bedroom was never rented out to anyone for an extended length of time. Mostly, it was used on occasion for the family when they visited.

This very room is where Mae would spend her final resting days. When she became very ill, they moved her into this space. She stayed with them up until her death. When family and friends came to visit her, they often stayed in furnished rooms on the same floor. I am uncertain as to what ultimately took my great-grandma's life; I do know my mom was not close to her as she never fully accepted her into their family and it was all because she did not share their German heritage.

Marie was one of the other boarders living on the second floor. There was no doubt that she left a lasting impression on Joni. She was tall and slender with long black curly hair the color of a raven that fell into a cascade of curls down her back, reaching almost to her waist. To just say that her eyes were blue was not enough. They were not just your ordinary blue or the color of the clear sky. Her eyes were striking, like dark blue sapphires, skin flawless like porcelain and no wrinkles. Lips were plump, and blood red with soft rosy cheeks and a delicate nose just slightly turned up. She had natural beauty and didn't need much makeup, just a hint of color that would give her a pop; she was perfection. Oh, how my mother envied her fancy dresses and spiked high heels!

Marie loved her shoes, and she had one pair of heels that were especially stunning. They were crimson Mary Jane's with a 3.5-inch stiletto heel and a thin strap. Those shoes had a bow on the back with three lovely flowers on the side, a slightly open toe that allowed her perfectly red painted toenails to peek out. Mom always wanted heels just like those and was impressed by the girly-girl ways. Mom eventually reached a height of six feet tall; she would have been six feet three and a half in those heels! In her eyes, Marie was the most beautiful woman ever. Grandma, in contrast, was a practical woman. She never wore makeup, and always had her hair neatly pulled back in the same fashion every day. Marie would frequently allow my mom in her room while she dressed, did her hair, and put on her makeup. My mom was just around the tender age of thirteen. Sometimes she would put a little makeup on Mom, but she always washed it off before she left her room, as Grandma would not have approved of it.

Mom kept a diary; it was 1949, hard to believe my sister and I found it, and she had it all these years. Maintaining a journal was something I tried many times in the past, but it seemed I never succeeded longer than a few months. Mom wrote in her diary religiously; some of her most cherished childhood memories were there. It was exciting to find this treasure; journaling is where most venting and secrets of the most intimate details about people's lives come to life. Mom wrote some of her recollections in her diary with just a few entries primarily telling her story of how she became infatuated with a particular boy; his name was Ardell. She apparently had quite a crush on him and longed for his affection.

She thought Marie could help with some advice on how to attract him. She would confide in Marie as well as her diary. Her journal, of course, was off limits for anyone to read as she made it clear writing in it, "Please do not read my diary because it is all about my things, thank you." I mean how sweet; for my mom, it was surely her dad, as God help the boy that would ever break her heart.

On one entry, dated July 13, 1949, it read: "Today Ardell asked me to the show. I may yet go I hope so. I am still wearing his ring. Tomorrow night I am going on a moonlight walk. Ardell is arriving alone, I hope Eunice can't come, I like her, but I don't want her to be around tomorrow night. I want to walk along beside Ardell, and I hope something will happen. I hope he kisses me. I think I am falling in young love."

I must assume that Eunice, and from the many other entries she wrote professing her young love for Ardell, she would tag along and spoil their alone time. Mom was sure Marie could help her dress up appealing to Ardell.

She talked about a time when Marie was getting ready to go somewhere, and she felt it had to be a special occasion because her dress was so elegant. My mom recounted, when it came to chic, this dress was just that; it felt like chiffon with a sheer swath of material, sparkling sequins, it stretched down to meet up with her sweetheart neckline. The elaborate strips of material ran up and down the dropped empire waist, with dreamy feathered accents.

As Marie was putting her makeup on, she allowed Mom to go through her closet. She was excited as her eyes glazed through so many fabulous dresses. As she was looking at all her gorgeous clothes, Marie encouraged her to try a dress on. Marie was a bit busty, and my mom was not. She thought to herself, none of her clothes would look good on her until she came across a fantastic black cocktail dress. Joni could not resist and had to try it on. It had a jewel-embellished neckline with fancy gathering and an off-the-shoulder design with cap sleeves, and a hemline that fell slightly above the knee. Does it make you swoon, darling? Those well-crafted capped sleeves were a stunner; a sensible curve silhouette that gathered and tailored to flatter her figure was perfect for her date. One of Mom's famous last words, "sensible," and this dress was just that.

Mom did have one thing going for her, as she was tall and slender. The way the dress gathered on her flat chest was flattering. As she slipped into the dress looking in the mirror, she suddenly felt like royalty. She could have pranced around in it all night, but Marie had to go once she finished getting ready.

Joni was unaware at the time she was having a conversation with a prostitute.

Joni asked, "Are you going to work?"

Marie cautiously explained, "Why yes, that is why I have to get moving along."

Joni moaned, "I wish you didn't have to go as I am having so much fun! When can I come back as I am going to a show with Ardell tomorrow and could use your beauty tip advice?"

Marie whispered in her ear, "I will be back in the morning, but I have to sleep so you can come by later in the day and I will help you get ready."

She made Mom feel extraordinary and lovely, all at the same time. Marie was special to her as she taught her unique beauty tips; it was their little secret. It was apparent to Grandma that Joni became infatuated with Marie's beauty secrets. Although Grandma knew her occupation, she made it quite clear to her not to tell Joni. I find it hard to believe she rented to her, but after all, Grandma was a businesswoman, and she didn't judge.

Growing up with Marie in the house made it so much fun for my mom. She told my mother she worked at a nearby five-star hotel as the hostess in this clean restaurant. The hotel was the Omni William Penn. This Pittsburgh hotel was built in 1916 and was known for its striking beauty and charming elegance. At the time, this made sense to Mom as to why she would get so glammed up. My mother was always confused as to why she slept during the day. Marie didn't elaborate on her work or what she did at the hotel, though most speculated she often danced in those fancy stiletto heels. I can't even imagine walking in those extremely high heels, let alone standing in them all night. Sometimes she would walk to work on nice days, and when she did, she would wear flat shoes and carry her heels in a bag; however, when the weather was bad, she took a cab. Mom figured she was wealthy and never seemed to want for anything as she always paid her rent on time.

At Christmas, many of the residents would give Joni little gifts; this pleased my grandmother. Marie's gifts were always Mom's favorite, as it was always something soft and silky, making her feel so girly. One gift mom always remembered was a pink chiffon scarf. Whenever she wore the silky wrap, she felt as though she just stepped out of a movie. It was just like Marie to show Mom how to tie it around her neck as well as in a ponytail.

She'd say, "Every girl should own a pink chiffon scarf. You should wear that scarf in a ponytail on a date with Ardell."

In the end, Marie rented from them for quite a few years. My grandmother knew all along Marie led a bit of an unconventional lifestyle, but she also knew how impressed Mom was with her. It wasn't until Marie finally left that Grandma told her she did not work at that fancy hotel. It's hard to explain the difference between a regular prostitute and a call girl to a child, but according to Grandma, Marie was a high-class prostitute. I suppose it means she catered to the wealthy. This hotel was fancy and plush, so I imagine that is why Marie set herself up in that establishment. Marie left when my mom was around fifteen. My mom never saw her again but never forgot her either.

Chapter 5

The Package

In the spring of 1949, a package came addressed to Joni; this package would forever change her life. As Mom recounted the story, she remembers sitting on the front porch, recovering from a tonsillectomy. Grandma was sitting with her as they enjoyed the breeze and all the flowers in bloom. Her throat was still sore from the surgery, but she was so happy that morning. She felt like a cherished princess tucked in her favorite glider porch swing. Joni had feathered cushions tucked all around her, which made for such a cozy, relaxing spot.

Grandma had just brought her a dish of ice cream to soothe her aching throat; now contented, she looked out at their quiet neighborhood. "Here comes Tom," she said. The beloved mailman, a good friend to everyone in their town, strode cheerfully down the sidewalk toward their house. Joni leaned forward eagerly, wondering if she would get any mail. Since she was recovering from a tonsillectomy, maybe, just perhaps, there would be a get-well card in the mail.

"Joni!" their mailman called. "I have a package for you."

A package, for Joni—this was better yet; she had never gotten a package in the mail before. Joni quickly sat up and leaned forward looking to see what Tom was bringing. He couldn't climb the front porch stairs fast enough, and Grandma looked somewhat puzzled, but Joni was so excited she stood up, knocking all the blankets that Grandma tucked around her onto the porch.

"Here you go, Joni." Tom handed her the package wrapped in brown paper, big enough to have something exciting inside. She sat back down on the glider eagerly tearing the brown paper off the box.

She was so excited her hands were shaking. "Mommy, a package for me, who could have sent it?"

As she looked over at her mother, there was a confused and anxious look on her face, which stopped her cold. She scooted up next to her, putting her arm around her and studied the return address on the paper.

"Joni, honey," Grandma said, her voice sounded tight, almost frightened. "It's from Iva, your birth mother."

Birth mother, she had almost forgotten she had any other mother than Dorothy, the mother sitting next to her with her arms wrapped around her in such a warm, loving way. Now, as she clutched the partially opened package on her lap, memories suddenly flooding back, memories she'd almost forgotten these last few years.

She recalled the time when she talked to her kindergarten teacher about coming to the Doyles with her suitcase because they needed her.

Whispered words from Dorothy's relatives about how she didn't belong. The confusion and puzzlement she felt each time one of the other little children used to stay at their house when she was little and went back to be with their mommies and daddies.

As she slowly opened the box, she could hear Dorothy, her mom, talking to her gently trying to explain to her about Iva, about the woman who had handed her over to my grandma when she was just a baby.

Joni didn't want to hear the words she was saying; she didn't want to think about another woman who was now trying to come back into her life. She folded the tissue paper inside the box back and saw a pink and gray plaid dress.

She jumped up and threw the dress to the ground; "No!" she shouted. "I don't want it, take it away!" By now, she was shaking all over.

Her daddy came out on the porch. "What is going on, what's all the shouting about?"

Grandma tried to explain to her, but she was scared, angry and out of control now, shouting over Grandma's words.

"She can't come back; she can't, I don't want anything from her. She's not my real mom."

"Joni Doyle," her father said firmly. "Go to your room until you can calm down!"

Sobbing, she ran into the house and downstairs to her room. How could this be happening? Just a few minutes ago, she was Frank and Dorothy's cherished daughter, and now she felt like Cinderella in her rags, sobbing with no one to love her. So many evil thoughts rushed through her head; what if Iva came back and took her away, where would she live, would she ever see her real Mom and Dad; Dorothy and Frank again?

She sat up on her bed wiping away her tears, swallowing against the rawness of her sore throat. Would they even want her now that she had acted like such a brat?

Joni looked out the back door from her room to the little-sheltered downstairs courtyard; she saw the chair her daddy often sat in and rocked for hours. Some nights when he could not sleep and Grandma could not find him, she would find him in his rocker. It seemed to calm him, to give him peace in the evenings. Joni went to the back of the house and sat in the rocker, upset and full of tears. Cautiously she opened the door and crept out, her eyes aching and swollen from all the crying. She began to settle herself in Daddy's rocker and began to rock, back and forth, back, and forth.

While Joni was calming herself, my grandparents saw there were several notes inside the box. One was attached to the dress for my mom, and the other addressed to Dorothy; the letter to Joni was short, reading:

"I have been ill, and I'm still not able to care for my little girl, but I honestly do care for you."

Joni read the note, and she became angry. To Mom, this meant Iva did exist, and she feared she might take her away from the Doyles; she didn't believe her. This woman had never tried to see her or even call her; now she was afraid she might just show up one day and demand to take her back.

There was the other letter with Dorothy's name on the envelope. My grandparents sat next to one another, and they stared at the packet with a strange look on their faces, questioning whether they should read it. A few minutes passed, and they agreed to open it. Grandma ripped the envelope and read it aloud to Frank.

"Dear Mrs. Doyle and my little girl. I guess you think I should be ashamed of myself, and honestly and truthfully, I am. You know I just cannot help thinking sometimes feeling how unfortunate it has been I have never been able to see Joni. This is the reason I do not write because I get so blue. I just would love to see her and hold her once again. I want you to know, I have thanked God so many times for you and her wonderful home. I would just have to cry if I called you and heard her voice, which I have been tempted many times to do. If God

answers my prayers, I will be able to get out to see you all this fall. I know she is great in her schoolwork if she takes after the other children. They are all getting along so well. I know I have started a dialogue of letters and I started crying then stop. I will finish tonight. Wasn't the war awful? My youngest brother was 36 years old though and was in Air Corp. at Wilmington Delaware. We missed him heaps. So many boys from Chamby (Chambersburg, PA) went and six within a half block right in our block here. The war took so many of our loved ones, and left so many people with such heartaches; Glad it is over. Mrs. Doyle, I know you could never help but think I'm a bad mother. I love Joni just as much as I do the children here. Only I cannot write and explain, and God has sure been kind to give me such a good home for her. I'd love to have a current snap-shot or camera picture that's all until I may someday again have a home of my own then I'll have you if you can come to see me. I'd love to talk to you. I've so much to tell you, and of course, I'd be so happy to see Joni. Give her my love and kisses and tell her to be a good little girl."
Gratefully Yours, Mrs. I.M. Goulding

I can't imagine what was going through my grandparent's minds after reading her correspondence. The circumstances, which led Iva to give my mother up in the first place, were so terribly sad. At this point in Joni's life, they were connected to her as if she were their natural born daughter. My mom was the light of their lives, and they were honored to be her parents.

As Dorothy thoughtfully finished reading the letter, she looked at Frank and said, "We can't read this to Joni, it will crush her."

"Well I do think she is old enough to understand the circum-stances which brought her to us, we need to have a talk with her and reassure her. It is important we are open so she can move forward and feel safe."

"I know you are right; it just breaks my heart when she fears Iva is coming to take her away. Quite frankly it concerns me; she just might come for her."

"Right, I don't want to, and I certainly don't want to hurt her, nor can I believe Iva would send this package unexpectedly. I too wonder if she will show up unannounced!" Dorothy reread the letter; she realized Frank was right. Joni deserved to know the truth. She so desperately needed their support.

They began looking for her, calling out, "Joni, where are you?"

Joni was rocking back and forth in her Daddy's rocker; she yelled, "I'm in the back sitting in Daddy's rocker."

As they approached, they found her crouched in the chair; it was apparent she was sad. "Oh Joni, we love you so much. I know this must be confusing to you, but nobody is taking you away from us—not now, not ever!"

Frank and Dorothy threw their arms around her. They could feel their daughter tremble with worry.

Joni was sobbing, "Why did she send me the dress, can't she just leave me alone?" Joni dabbed at her tears trailing down her cheek, "I don't want to keep wondering if she will ever come for me, I just want her to leave me alone."

"We don't want you to worry, just let us do the worrying," Dorothy assured her.

It pained them to see how scared she was.

She clung to her mommy and daddy, "Promise, you promise she will leave me alone?"

Grandma gently whispered in her ear, "Shhhh, everything is going to be all right, she is just checking on you that's all. She is not going to take you away. In her letter, she wrote how fortunate she is for your daddy and me to give you such a loving home. Now that doesn't sound like someone who plans to take you away."

Joni rubbed her swollen eyes as the sunshine streamed down on her face. Joni sat up and looked at her mommy and daddy; she felt a sense of relief as if the world faded away and drained away all her fear. Joni would no longer think about Iva anymore. My mom did not want any part of the dress. To this day, she doesn't know what happened to the dress, but Grandma never mentioned it again. I am confident she donated it to someone who needed it more than my mom did.

Dorothy decided not to read the letter to Joni because she knew it would only confuse her even further, as Iva did mention at some point she wanted to come and see her. I am sure this note was a way for her to try to reconnect with her daughter. This situation, however, was a wake-up call for my grandparents as they realized they were not her legal guardians.

Once they finally could calm Joni down, she went downstairs to her room to lie down. Frank and Dorothy went back to the front porch and pondered her letter again.

Dorothy questioned her comment, "Why would she wait so long to write, and why shouldn't I think poorly of her, she gave her to us when she was just five days old, and she is now thirteen."

Frank explained to her with sorrow, "We have to be strong for Joni; I don't want her to feel scared. We have to show her she is ours, so let's adopt her."

Dorothy was in full agreement, "You are right, we have dragged our feet for too long. It's time we ensure our little girl will never have to worry again."

I know Grandma didn't think badly of Iva. Grandma's treasure was her daughter, and she loved her more than her life. As for my mom, I know she loved her the very day Iva placed her in their arms.

Being given away isn't easy by any means, but as Mom once told me, "What I know for sure, no matter how I came to the Doyles, they were my mom and dad, and their love ran just as deep as if they were my biological parents."

As a mother myself, words can't describe the unconditional love I have for my children. My mother was not just my mom; she was my best friend. I cannot comprehend the notion of giving your child away but had Iva not done so, who knows what might have happened. Grandma sympathized with the sadness Iva evidently felt having to give Joni up, but at the same time, she recognized they had to take a stance and fight for her!

Attempted Adoption

Reflecting on this significant event in their lives leads me to believe this package was indeed a wake-up call for my grandparents. They decided to investigate further the possibility of legally adopting my mother, so they contacted a lawyer in Harrisburg, Pennsylvania. My mom always knew that Frank and Dorothy were not her biological parents. They never hid it from her, and when I asked how old my mom was when she realized she was not theirs, she didn't know.

She stated, "I can't recall the first moment I knew, I just always knew. My parents are my parents, and it doesn't change how I feel about them, even though my birth mother abandoned me. I don't feel alienated or different as I had the best parents in the whole world!"

One of the boarders worked as a legal aid, and my grandparents decided to get her advice on what steps to take in adopting my mom. Her name was Dottie, and she referred them to an attorney by the name of Mary Bush. That license plate number

Frank had written down the day they first met Iva served to be extremely helpful in finding Iva.

That morning, while getting ready to meet Mrs. Bush, my grandparents frantically were making sure they had all the necessary paperwork for my mother's adoption.

As Dorothy was getting ready, she yelled out to Frank, "We have to hurry; we don't want to miss the train."

"I'm ready to go; I will check on Joni and see if she is as well." He didn't want to admit it, but he was nervous, as this was the first time, they would see Iva since all those years ago when she handed Joni over to them. Frank yelled, "Joni, are you ready, as we have to catch the train?"

Joni was patiently waiting in her room, "Yes, I'm all set, are we finally leaving?"

Dottie so kindly volunteered to drive them to the train station. Mom had never been on a train before. She was excited about her first train ride but scared to meet Iva face-to-face, not to mention how terrified she was of what she might encounter when she met her.

When they arrived at the railway station, it was early in the morning. Crowds had started gathering at the ticketing counter, and the lines were long. Fortunately, they had already bought their tickets a few days in advance, so they went straight to the platform to wait for their train.

The train finally arrived, and they scrambled into their seats. My mom was lucky to get a seat by the window. At last, the conductor came around and took everyone's tickets. As the train began to move, there was a loud Wooo, Wooo whistle sound, almost like a forlorn call in the night. Mom was so excited to ride on the train and has spoken of how she enjoyed the jerky movement it made.

The scenery outside was beautiful. It seemed while Joni was gazing out the window, she was able to forget about the meeting looking at the beautiful trees and flowers. Everyone on the train was friendly, and she could hear the other passengers talking and joking amongst themselves. What she didn't expect was how many times the train would make a stop for other passengers to get on. The engines hissed, and the brakes squeaked each time they would come to a halt; once everyone boarded the train, it began to move again. Then it started to accelerate to a constant speed.

Finally, the train jolted to a complete stop. The passengers, Joni and her mom and dad, had finally reached their destination as they placed their feet on the ground. Upon their arrival in Harrisburg, they quickly got a cab to take them to meet with the attorney, Mrs. Mary Bush. She had a law office in the courthouse right in the center of town.

As Mrs. Bush was introducing herself to everyone, she didn't have the best of news to deliver to them, "I am sorry to have to tell you, but it appears that Iva will not be attending our meeting today."

"What! Why is she not going to be here today, are you saying we came all this way for nothing?"

Joni was upset as she felt her motive in not showing up was because she would not allow the Doyles to adopt her, even though she agreed to meet with them. Much to everyone's surprise who came in her place was Iva's father, my mom's biological grandfather, Mr. Alexander.

Mrs. Bush then explained, "Before you get too worried, Iva's father is here in her place. Unfortunately, he doesn't have the authority to sign the adoption papers."

"I don't understand are you telling us we cannot adopt Joni."

"Yes and no, it is a bit more complicated, but before you get too upset, you need to hear what Iva's father has to say."

Joni, along with Frank and Dorothy, was so confused. If Iva was the only person who had the power to sign the adoption papers, then how could she be adopted?

"Okay, he is in the room next door; I am going to introduce you to him so he can explain why Iva is not here today."

As the anticipation was building, they sat patiently in their chairs while she went to get Mr. Alexander. Their faces turned to the door when they heard his voice. There was a lingering sense of awkwardness as Mrs. Bush introduced him to them.

As my mother looked at him, she was trying to see any resemblance she might have with him. He was an ordinary framed man, tall, wearing a gray wool button-up sweater, a billed cap, and his face looked kind; however, she could see only a hint of a likeness. As he settled in his chair, he seemed to look at my mother lovingly. Still, though, I think he realized his boundaries, as he was meeting his granddaughter for the first time, and didn't want to startle my mom.

"Hello, I know you were expecting Iva today, but she is not well, so I came in her place. I know this must be tough for all of you, and by the looks on your faces, I want to put your mind at ease." Iva's father explained.

"So exactly what is it you are trying to tell us, we are all Joni knows as her parents, and she would be devastated if you or Iva would take her away from us."

"I feel Joni should remain in your care. She is so fortunate to have such loving people as you caring for her. The last thing I want to do is take her away from a loving and stable environment. Iva is in no position to care for Joni. In fact, she has difficulty caring for the other four children she already has." Mr. Alexander was firm in his assertion.

One would think the Doyles could move forward and make it official by signing the adoption papers, but not so. Iva did not consent to an adoption to relinquish Joni to the Doyle's; I think she thought one day my mom might want to form a relationship with her and was hopeful she would be able to take her back. I can't even grasp how difficult this must have been for her, but I am so grateful my mom remained in the care of the Doyles. They never were able to adopt her formally. She returned home with them, and they continued to live their lives just as they always had.

As my mom related the story to me, she remembered how saddened her grandfather was by the overall situation; because he was not only meeting her for the first time, he knew he might never see her again. I wonder if not showing up was Iva's intent because maybe in her mind she knew my mom was better off with the Doyle's. I would speculate it would have been too painful for her to see Joni.

Mrs. Bush then explained, "The good news is Joni will remain under your care, but the bad news is since we do not have Iva's consent, you are not able to legally adopt her. You can take Joni home, and as Mr. Alexander has promised, she will continue to live with you forever."

As they were wrapping up the meeting, Mr. Alexander could see the worry on Joni's face. It was apparent to him he needed to reassure her, "I don't want you ever to have to be concerned with the notion of being removed from your home. You are one lucky little girl, and it is obvious the right thing for all of us here today is to consider your happiness."

She felt a terrible weight lifted off her shoulders as she crumpled on her chair lifting her head up to acknowledge his kind words.

A single tear rolled down her cheek with a slight grin on her face, relieved she was going home with the Doyles, "Thank you, I am happy with my mommy and daddy." Joni said.

It was at that moment she realized she would never fear the

thought of Iva taking her away. Once again, Joni was blessed; she met her grandfather that day!

Frank and Dorothy always considered my mom as their own, so it never mattered to her what others might think since they were not able to complete the adoption. I believe she was happy just to belong and have their devotion and dedication.

Sometime later, when Joni was a bit older, she learned she had three brothers and one sister: twins Jerry and Joyce, and Jim and Jack. The thought of having siblings was strange to her. Shortly after that meeting, a second package came in the mail with a photo of Iva and her siblings. When she received the envelope, she pondered whether or not she wanted to open it. To open or not, was the question.

This envelope was arguably an important element in her life. Grandma was curious, but she wanted it to be Joni's decision. "Should I open it?"

"It's up to you, but I think you will wonder what's in the packet if you don't."

"I guess you are right."

She began ripping it open with her digits, slid her hand inside, and pulled out the paper.

"What's it say?"

"Oh!" A tingling sensation ignited her fingertips as she unfolded the letter. "Joni, what's wrong?"

She could barely answer, as it was a photo wrapped in a piece of paper. "It's a picture of Iva and my brothers and sister."

For the first time, she was putting a face to their names. She leaned over, shared the photo with Dorothy, and pointed to everyone as described in the letter. "It seems so bizarre to finally see how they all look. I can stop the wondering, but it doesn't change the fact they are strangers to me."

Back left to right: Jim Goulding, Jerry Goulding, Jack Goulding
Front left to right: Iva Goulding and Joyce Goulding

She never really liked looking at the picture. As powerful as that moment was for my mother, she just had a hard time accepting them as her family.

Mother did her best to explain to me all that had transpired at the meeting in Harrisburg, along with the how and why she didn't worry about being taken away after the meeting. The anguish she must have felt had to have tortured her over the years and made her wonder if she was safe. It makes me appreciate the unconditional love my parents gave to both my sister and me.

Grandma would always say she was my mom's foster mother, which was true. Unfortunately, Joni didn't have any legal papers to prove this and no one ever asked. If anyone did ask what my mom's full name was, Grandma would say "Joan Helen Goulding Doyle." It was a long name, but my mom was glad it ended with the last name Doyle; having the last name Doyle was important to her.

Chapter 6

First Job

Within a couple of years, Joni began to seriously consider being a nurse, just like her mother Dorothy, who was Mom's "Florence Nightingale." She was probably around fifteen years old when she applied for her first job at Shadyside Hospital where Grandma worked. Mom recounted the story about her first interview; she felt lucky. Grandmother had been employed there and there was the possibility of some great contacts for her. On the day of her interview, she was early. To say that some people pride themselves on being on time would be an understatement for Mother. The importance of being on time for her was over the top! It was everything to her and a habit she instilled in both my sister and me. I am the prompt twin, whereas, as much as my sister strives to be punctual, it is just not in her DNA, ha-ha—but that is my sissy! I can remember Mom purposely telling Connie to arrive at a particular time; if there were a family dinner, she would typically tell her to come fifteen minutes early to ensure she arrived on time.

On the day of her interview, she made sure she was well-dressed. It was a sunny day with a brisk wind blowing. It was early spring, but it almost felt like winter! She sheltered her face with a scarf. As she was approaching the front door to the hospital, she thought to herself about what might happen. Perhaps she would get the job that day, and they would want her to start the same day! She so wanted to make a good impression.

When she finally arrived, she quickly approached the reception desk where she announced her arrival. Due to her punctuality, she was nearly thirty minutes early. The receptionist said, "You are a little early, have a seat, and I will let the boss know you are here." Joni respectfully replied, "okay, thank you," and swiftly sat in a nearby empty seat in the lobby.

She was a new face in a hallway full of people and felt very nervous. She noticed a few people staring at her, and so she gazed back at them. One thing for certain, my mother was not shy. Gradually, people strolled into the lobby, and a young fellow sat next to her. My mom was not sure if he was a patient or someone waiting to interview as well.

He was curious to find out why my mom was there, so he spoke out and began talking to her, "What are you doing here, are you visiting someone?"

"No, I am waiting to interview for a position in the dietary department, I want to be a registered nurse someday, just like my mother," Joni replied.

The man smiled back, "That is an honorable career path, but why do you want to work in the dietary department?"

"You have to start somewhere, right?" Joni replied.

"Yes, I suppose you are correct."

There she sat, anxiously waiting for the hiring manager to call her name. "Joan Doyle" a woman bellowed her name.

Joni instantly jumped up out of her chair and introduced herself. "I'm Joan Doyle, how are you today?"

"Fine, fine, we will be meeting in my office; follow me, she replied."

As Mother strolled behind her, she noticed how polished her attire was. She had on a lovely blue dress with a tailored jacket. I remember Mom impressing upon me that a first impression is everything; stand tall, smile, and make sure you are groomed and dressed well. My mother was a beautiful, tall, statuesque woman; she was dressed in a conservative, simplistic, blue dress that was cinched at the waist.

"Good morning, Joan, I am the hiring manager and my name is Nancy."

"Good morning,"

"How are you today?"

"I am doing very well, thank you."

"I hope you didn't have any trouble getting here."

"No, not at all."

"Okay, great let's start the interview, are you ready?"

"Yes, I am."

It was a typical interview, according to my mother; her first question was, "Please tell me a little bit about yourself and why you think you are a good fit for the job." This initial question seemed to break the ice, and from that point on, the conversation went smoothly.

"I am eager to work in the hospital, and my hopes and dreams are to follow my mother's footsteps into nursing."

"Well, this job will be working in the dietary department, not the most glamorous position. You will be preparing trays for patients and washing the dishes. How does that sound to you?"

"Oh, I understand, and I would be grateful for the opportunity. I am a fast learner, and I know I will do a good job. I feel this is a great start for me to work in a hospital."

She was hired right on the spot. She didn't start work that day, but a few days later, she was being trained in the dietary department passing out trays that consisted of special diets for the patients. Thinking back, what she remembered most about the experience was seeing all the very ill patients. She always tried to talk with them in hopes to cheer them up. She knew being a nurse was what she wanted to do, and I truly believe it was her calling, as anyone who encountered "Nurse Joni" will tell you; she was loved by all.

As much as she hated seeing all the sick patients and smelling that hospital smell, strangely, she was comfortable there. She remembered some of her co-workers being disgusted by the scent, insisting the hospital smell was too overpowering for some of her colleagues. The smell seemed to stick in the back of their throats, as they would describe some of the noxious hospital smells. For Mother, as she walked through the halls, the smell of sickness, helplessness, confusion, fear, and uncertainty that flooded their senses didn't bother her at all. For her, it was a place that was sparkling clean and sunny, and she tried to make a difference every day and hoped in some way her presence made someone smile in his or her time of illness. She never understood what all the fuss was about.

She worked in the dietary department for approximately a year and decided she wanted to venture out into direct patient care. She was sixteen and still in high school when she applied for a position as a nurse's aide at the Eye and Ear Hospital. Working with patients certainly tested her abilities and patience of what it was like to care for sick people. Once she began that job, it gave her the experience and understanding needed to solidify her decision in becoming a nurse.

Mom was very excited when she was assigned to work on the pediatric floor. She loved working with children of all ages, especially the babies. She was not really sure at that time what specialty she wanted to study in nursing, but she was thrilled to be working in the field in whatever the capacity; for her, it was gratifying to be helping sick people.

A story that my mom recounted to me resonates as she felt like this was her calling being able to help an innocent child in a desperate situation. Joni was walking by a patient's room, and she suddenly heard someone crying. This immediately caught her attention stopping her dead in her tracks. She quickly ran into the room and discovered a little boy, who apparently had Scarlet Fever, who was crying with big tears streaming down his face. Mother felt so sorry for him. Joni did her best to reassure him he was going to be all right; because mom was a nurse's assistant, protocol stated a registered nurse had to be called. When she softly touched his forehead, he was burning up with fever. Scary, she thought, but she remained "cool as a cucumber." I remember when she recounted this story to me and how impressed I was, as she was only sixteen at the time.

The boy's mother was sitting by his side, and she was beside herself with worry. "You have to help my son; he is burning up, please do something!" his mother blurted. Mom's instinct was to immediately get a cold washcloth and place it on his forehead. She can remember her mother doing the same for her when she was running a temperature.

"Let's try to cool him down with an icy washcloth."

She then rushed to get a cold rag, dampened it with water as cold as she could get it, and gently patted his face. She then told his mother to hold it in place while she found a nurse. It made me think back to the first time I heard the words, "Scarlet Fever" in a famous children's book, *The Velveteen Rabbit* where the little boy is stricken with this disease. The little boy in the hospital that day was nursed back to health, and my mother felt she played a key role in his recovery. Mom intrinsically knew working with babies was special, as they don't possess the power of speech; once again, she played a vital role in acting as his voice, helping him heal.

Mom was blessed that while she worked as a nurse's aide, she was awarded the opportunity to float from floor to floor which gave her a different perspective on not just caring for pediatric patients, but adults and geriatrics. It was fascinating to her to see the differences in the level of patient care for all age groups. She knew this experience led her to working in a private family practice clinic; she was able to help people of all ages.

We all have friends that we meet along the way who become our lifelong friends. Barbara Johnson happened to be that friend to my mom. Although they did not know each other in high school, they met at the Eye and Ear Hospital, the year was 1952, and they were both sixteen years old. Mom had been there before Barbara's start date, and now Mom was assigned to the operating room.

Your first day of work can be incredibly intimidating; for Barbara, she began on the right foot. Their former boss at the time, Mrs. Eichenger led her to my mom, who as it came to be, would become her best friend forever.

"We just recently hired another gal, she is tall, like you; I think the two of you will do just fine together." Mrs. Eichenger said. Joni was tall just like Barbara; both were nearly six feet tall. It would have been expected that Mrs. Eichenger would have taken the time to introduce the two of them, but for whatever reason, she chose not to. Barbara just wanted to survive her first day at her new job; she wasn't completely sure working in an operating room was her forte. Barbara didn't really have a clear plan of what her career path might be after high school graduation. She eventually decided to take Mrs. Eichenger's advice and track down the tall girl. She was excited, but nervous, at the same time, thinking, how am I going to remember everything?

When she found the operating room, her attention was immediately drawn to a tall, thin-framed girl; she knew immediately she must be Joni. Mom was cleaning some of the surgical instruments.

Barbara approached her and said, "Hi, my name is Barbara, this is my first day. While I was in orientation with Mrs. Eichenger, she told me you started working here not too long ago, and you could show me around."

Joni was so thrilled to meet someone her age, "Yes, my name is Joan, but everyone calls me Joni; are you going to be working in the surgery unit?"

"Yes, I am, it looks like we will be working together."

During the first few days, Mom introduced Barbara to everyone; the two seemed to instantly bond the moment they met. The operating room was a fun and exciting place for my mom to work and she was excited to explore the different responsibilities that it entailed. Barbara, on the other hand, wasn't so sure if she would fit in, as she was still trying to figure out what she wanted to do. It saddened her to see all the sick patients, especially those that didn't make it.

I truly believe it takes a special kind of person to be a nurse and not everyone is cut out for it. I admire Barbara for eventually realizing that it does take a particular set of talents, interests, personality traits, and passion for being a nurse. She saw early on that my mom had all those unique combinations of attributes to be a successful registered nurse.

Barbara was like the sister Mom never had. Saying she was my mom's best friend was an understatement. They were always there for one another, and Barbara was like the missing puzzle piece of my mom's life that I believe she had been searching for all through high school and found her in the hospital of all places.

They certainly didn't agree on everything and what most close friends encounter in their lifetime is conflict. There was a time where they didn't agree with their religious beliefs, and this situation was a major blowout, to say the least. I think that occasionally fighting with your friend is normal, as any two people in a friendship are going to disagree from time to time. However, they regretted their silly spat and found themselves deeply missing each other. I suppose we all need some time to cool off and in their case; they needed six weeks.

The experience my mother gained by working on the surgical floor gave her the ambition to become a surgical nurse along with great examples my grandma set in place for her. Barbara remained my mother's friend up until she passed and she graciously took on the role as Auntie to my sister and me. She is our family!

Both my mother and Auntie Barb, (that's what we called her), graduated from high school in 1953. Dorothy and Frank were so proud of Mom, who graduated in February of 1953; Auntie Barb graduated in June of 1953. Graduating in February seems a little odd, but Mom started her senior year in June and Auntie Barb in September. The last day of high school for my mom was finally here. After graduation, some people experience an uncertainty of what to do next, but not my mom, she was already enrolled in the nursing program, which was slated to begin the following month; there was no such thing as taking time off for my mother.

Nurse's Training

In March of 1953, my mother went away to nursing school. It was difficult for her to say goodbye to my grandma and grandpa; she had never been away from home. It was a memorable day when my mom's daddy took her to her dorm, the place she would call home for the next three years. As with most freshmen starting college, she was terrified of fitting in with her peers and leaving home. Mom found it very difficult not having her best friend there, as she didn't know anyone. Mom did a lot of wondering about what kind of roommate she might be paired with; there were so many questions: What if she didn't get along with her roomie, what if she got homesick? She was extremely nervous and excited all at the same time.

When she walked into her assigned room, she was surprised by how small it was; there were two twin beds, one under the only window, and the other was near the door. She was assigned the bed under the window. There was only one dresser, and it was to be shared with her roommate. Mom's room at home was a bit small, but it was all hers. Her bedroom was a tiny alcove just off the kitchen. It was in the basement, and the walls needed finishing. She didn't have your traditional lath and plaster walls as you often saw back in those days. There was a single bathroom in the basement where she grew up, and she shared with her parents. Of course, now she would be sharing a common bathroom with many other students. As far as a closet—well, it was located at the end of the hall outside the room, and she shared it with many of the other students. She did not take many clothes with her, as every day she had to wear a nurse's uniform as well as a cap while working on the hospital floors.

Finally, after a few minutes alone in her dorm room, her roomie walked in. When Mom met her, she politely approached her and shook her hand, "Hi, my name is Joni and yours?" She seemed shy, as she put her head down when she reached for her hand, "Hello, my name is Becky." Becky was short compared to my mother's six-foot tall, thin frame. As Becky looked up, my mom noticed a scar on the right side of her face. She thought to herself, how sad to be so young and live with a scar so prominent. It wasn't huge, but it was noticeable. It appeared that the mark on her face embarrassed her.

Becky had long brown hair with a far-right-side part. When she looked up, she had the most incredible shade of blue eyes. Her eyes were steel blue that reminded Mother of a calm but confident person. She wore very little makeup; just enough to cover her blemish and highlight her high cheekbones, and a soft nude color lip. Becky was very vibrant and full of positive energy, once people became friends with her the scar was virtually invisible.

During their conversation, Becky explained, "You're probably wondering why I wear such a far-right-side part in my hair draped over my cheek, it's because I am trying to cover my scar."

"Oh . . . well, I don't want you to feel uncomfortable with a bunch of questions, but I suppose I was curious about how you got the scar."

"Well, my mom was cooking fried chicken, and I wanted to help; when she turned to tidy up the kitchen, I reached up to the frying pan with a spatula in my hand and attempted to flip the chicken. The pot slid off the burner, hit the floor and grease splashed out and hit my face. I think I was around six or seven years old. My mom tells me I am fortunate that the hot oil didn't splash in my eyes."

Mom was mortified and felt such sympathy for Becky, "OH MY GOSH; I'm so glad you are OK! I'm sure your mother was so scared for you."

"Yes, she was, but it was an accident. I suppose it could have been worse." Becky replied.

Apparently, once they got that somewhat awkward moment out of the way, they began discussing their families and where they went to high school along with their desires in what led them to become a nurse. After a few minutes of talking, they learned they had a lot in common. Mom was so relieved with the ease of their conversation and happy to have her as her roomie.

A negative aspect of where their room was situated in the hallway was that it was at the opposite end from where the bathrooms and showers were located. Mom used to hate it when she would have to get up out of bed to go pee in the middle of the night, as she would have to traipse down that long hallway.

They had a dorm mother who watched all of them. She was diligent about doing a room check every night at 9:00 pm sharp. She made it near impossible to sneak out at night, and my mom's parents always taught her to play by the rules, so the thought of sneaking out was the furthest thing from her mind—so she thought!

Working and all that studying seemed like a good excuse to get out on a Friday night and have a little fun. First, they had to plan a way to get out of the dorms without being caught. They figured out a way to escape from the boiler room where no one would see them. One night after their dorm mother did her usual bed check, some of my mom's friends, along with Becky, gathered in their room to come up with a plan to sneak out to a nearby bar. Oh, what fun they had at that bar. There were two other girls including my mother and Becky that successfully escaped the dorm, and off to the bars they went.

It was a risky endeavor on their part because if they were caught the consequences were either being suspended or worse—kicked out! I suppose the notion of bending the rules made the whole experience that much more exciting to them. That night they all made a pact they would stick together no matter what the circumstances. Once they arrived at the bar, they were surprised to see how many young, cute guys were there. Mom being the tallest, the girls nominated her as their leader to navigate them through the crowd towards the bar so they could order a drink.

At the time, Mom's drink of choice was a cranberry vodka spritzer. As they all got their drinks, they meandered in a sea of people searching for a spot where they could perch themselves to people watch, or in their case look for some cute boys. The bar was quite lively and throbbing, which only heightened their sense of naughtiness. You had to raise your voice to be heard over the music. As the girls were finally getting comfortable, they began swaying their hips back and forth, hoping a handsome young man would approach them and ask permission to dance.

Becky was laughing and enjoying herself; when she leaned over, Mom could smell wine on her breath. She pointed her finger at a guy she wanted to approach, "When I finish my drink, I'm going to march over and ask him to dance," Becky said.

It was evident that liquid courage gave her the needed bravery to approach the young man. Becky took her last sip and handed the glass to Mom and off she went.

"Hi, I'm Becky, are you having fun?" Becky yelled.

"Yeah, you?" The young man replied.

"Oh yes, some of my friends and I snuck out of the dorm for some fun, would you like to dance?"

"Sure, if you don't mind my horrible dance moves." He grabbed Becky's hand and guided her across the dance floor; nothing else seemed to matter, even though neither one of them could dance. Becky didn't care; he went right, she went right. If he sped up, she sped up. She figured she would do her best and follow along. When the song ended, they went their separate ways to opposite sides of the dance floor.

Then there was a sudden unexpected tap on my mom's shoulder. "Would you like to dance with me?"

She hesitated as she looked up at him. He was slightly taller than my mom was. "I would love to, but I don't know how to dance." Joni blushed.

"Well, that makes two of us, because I don't dance all that well, but I am sure we can figure it out."

He put her at ease, and Joni obligingly accepted his offer. The jukebox was playing an Elvis Presley song, "Love Me Tender." Oh no, she thought, it was a slow song. The young man turned gracefully, his body in tune with the slow-paced music. Joni was so flattered he asked her to dance, but he underestimated himself, as he was actually quite a skilled dancer. She didn't quite care at that moment. He placed his hand on her back, her hand was on his shoulder, and then their free hands met; together, they danced to the music, their feet moving somewhat coordinated. Joni's heart was beating so fast, and as the song progressed, she felt more relaxed and allowed a big smile to form on her lips. She couldn't help but think how handsome he was; Mom felt she was very special to get to dance with a partner like him. She never saw him again after that night, but it was a night to remember.

The girls had been having so much fun; the time had escaped them when they realized it was time to get back to the dorm before being discovered missing. As they were walking back to the dorms feeling no pain, the reality of being caught set in, and then the possibility of being suspended alarmed all of them; they were most definitely scared. As they made their way to the entrance of the boiler room, they spotted a couple of medical interns through the hospital window talking with a night nurse, they all knew them, as they worked on the same floors. To get their attention, they each grabbed some pebbles and tossed them to the window. One of the interns that Mom had a crush on came outside. "What are you girls doing out at this hour?" They all started whispering to each other trying not to be heard; the intern said in a demanding soft voice: "Please, one at a time; again, what are you all doing outside of your dorm rooms this late at night?"

Becky said, "We have all been studying and working so hard we just wanted a fun night out, so we went to the bar on the corner. Can you just help us get back in the dorm quietly?"

Of course, what went through Mom's mind was how upset her father would be if she were caught. She then pleaded: "You have to help us; my dad will kill me, please!"

"No, I am not getting involved, if you get caught I will get implicated in helping you, you girls are on your own." With that, he turned and walked away; they were in total disbelief he wouldn't assist them in. "What a jerk," Mom thought to herself.

Her thoughts of him being nice quickly faded. The girls moved forward with their original plan to go through the boiler room. They knew it was important to be extremely careful, as sometimes the security guard would position himself in a quiet spot to take a nap. Before they approached the door, they all thought of a plan to try to divert him if he were to awaken.

The girls then decided to mess up their hair as if they had been lying in bed studying. They were hoping the guard would believe that by the looks of their bed-heads, they were up late and the reason they went outside was to get some much-needed fresh air. As they approached the door ever so quietly, they inched their way around the corner, and quietly placed their feet on the ground to minimize any sound; tiptoeing across the floor staring at their feet, and as they looked up, there sat the security guard half-asleep in a chair.

They all stopped dead in their tracks, one by one like a domino effect. Mom motioned with her finger to her lips so the others would be quiet. They continued to gently walk by him on the pristine tiles, paying attention to every footstep while tiptoeing with the utmost care hoping he wouldn't wake up. The room was dimly lit. They listened intently for any other sounds in the dorm; there was not a sound, it was as if you could hear a pin drop!

Not one sound did they make as they lifted their feet to take another step, but then the security guard began to move. They started to run, and just as they were making their way to the stairs, he woke up; oh, holy moly! He quickly opened his eyes and jumped to his feet; he waved his finger in shame at them saying what they all knew exactly what he was going to say! "You girls are out past your curfew, looking at his watch and pointing; it's 2:00 am; need I remind your curfew is 9:00 pm. Not sure how you are going to explain this to the dorm mother."

They pleaded with him not to tell the dorm mother and tried to explain to him they had been studying. Becky said in a soft tone, "We just went out the front door to get some fresh air and the door locked behind us, seriously! Please don't tell."

Of course, he didn't for a second believe their story, and he turned all of them into the dorm mother; all the fun that evening was lost after that. They were caught, not just for breaking curfew but for drinking as well. At that moment, Mom's whole body was overcome with fear, to the point where she couldn't control her breathing, and she was having trouble taking in the air. She began to panic as she buried her face in her hands sobbing, tears streaming down her face:

"Becky, my parents are going to be so disappointed; what are we going to do?" Becky wrapped her arms around her, hoping to comfort her: "It's our first offense, we have good grades, I am sure we will all be just fine, we have to be!"

She didn't say another word; tears continued to roll down her cheeks. She couldn't fathom what just happened. Becky gently placed her hand on her back as they were escorted back to their dorm, and for a moment, she thought everything was going to be okay.

The next morning, Frank and Dorothy were called along with the other girl's parents. I think what was harder on my mom was

Joni upon completion of nurses' training

hearing the disappointment in her daddy's voice. If there was one thing she never wanted to do, it was to dishearten him. The thought of upsetting him was punishment enough for her!

That following Monday, the girls all met with a committee, who would determine their penance. All of them prayed they would not be suspended or even worse, thrown out!

God or somebody must have been watching over them because none of them were suspended or booted out of school.

They were grounded and under lock and key for two weekends. What a relief, they certainly learned a lesson the hard way as we all do growing up. One thing was for sure, for the remainder of her time in school she never left the grounds past 9:00 pm ever again. They found other ways to have a little fun. They would sneak out on the fire escape from time to time, as smoking was prohibited in their rooms, but it was always before 9:00 pm. It seemed in the1950s everybody smoked, even those in healthcare. Although Mom was not very rebellious, she tried to pick up smoking to fit in, and it seemed that back in the day it made you feel sophisticated. My mom didn't even know how to inhale a cigarette properly, but by golly, my mom was going to look cool just like everyone else! She gradually sucked some of the smoke in her mouth, held it in for a few seconds, and then she blew it all out at once. Oh, she thought she was so cool puffing away on a cigarette while telling stories out on the fire escape. Luckily, they were never caught.

Chapter 7

The Phone Call

Unbeknownst to Mom or my grandparents, Joni's birth mother, Iva, would keep track of her whereabouts as she grew and got older. Outside of the package that Iva sent her when she was younger, neither she nor any of the other biological family members ever attempted any contact with her. One evening, during her second year of nursing school, she was sitting in her dorm room doing homework when the phone rang in the dormitory on the main floor; anytime the phone rang, it was exciting, as there was only one phone for the entire dorm and all the students shared it.

There was a bellowing of a voice, "Joan Doyle, you have a phone call."

She wondered who it could be as she just talked with her mother and father, Joni answered the phone, and began to tremble a bit inside as the woman on the other end of the line announced she was Iva, her birth mother; there was a long pause between them.

Joni had never heard this woman's voice before; all those years ago, when she received the package with the dress, she had already dealt with the reality that she was not the Doyle's biological daughter, but now, hearing the woman's voice made it a reality. Joni wondered immediately how Iva knew where to find her. I can only imagine how creepy that must have been for her, realizing she'd watched her over the years. The world fell away for that moment in time, and Mom was lost for words, her dismay quickly turned to anger towards herself for answering the call.

Joni replied, "Hello," There was a brief silence, "Hello is anyone there?" Joni said.

"Uhhh . . . hello, this is Iva, I am your birth mother."

No, she thought to herself, my mother is Dorothy Doyle. Joni's stomach churned as she began talking.

"I am calling you as one of your brothers, Jerry, is getting married in a couple of days. I want you to come and meet your siblings and me of course."

Joni was trembling as she crouched down in the hallway with the phone in her hand, "Not sure if I can get time away from school; I need to call my mom and dad before I would consider going."

I can't imagine going to a wedding where you know no one, and the groom just happens to be a brother you have never met.

Iva pleaded, "Please come, I want you to meet everyone, and I am dying to hug you."

Joni was scared; she plopped herself down on the floor before she fell, "Again, I have to call my mom and dad, and I just don't know if I can get away. I will have to get back to you."

Iva implored one last time, "I want to see you before I get too old, and I want to meet you. I don't want to have any regrets of never trying to connect with you before I die." I shudder to think what was going through my mom's mind. She must have been tremendously frantic; she couldn't get off the phone fast enough.

"I will let you know if I am able or not. Goodbye."

Iva then said, "I have already arranged for your brother Jack to pick you up."

"Again, I am unsure, and I can't give you an answer right now, OK, I am hanging up now, bye-bye."

The only person she had met at this point was her biological grandfather, and although he was nice to her, that was enough for her.

"Goodbye, I will call you back tomorrow, is that all right?"

"Yes, I suppose, OK, goodbye."

She didn't know what to think or say at that moment; she needed time to gather her thoughts. So many questions flooded through her head: would her mother and father be upset with her, could she even get away from school, aside from Jack, do any of the other siblings know she even existed? There were so many unknowns. She knew it would be incredibly awkward for her parents to attend, and didn't know if they would even agree to go with her. Iva seemed to have it all planned out.

After hanging up with Iva, she was not convinced going to the wedding was a good idea. She was nineteen, legally an adult and realized Iva could not force her to go either. No matter what her master plan was, she could not change how she felt about the Doyles. In her heart, they were her family. Of course, there was always a sense of curiosity of where she came from, and this voice she was hearing validated this woman existed.

She immediately dialed Grandma; Grandmother was just as surprised to hear Iva contacted her; however, she had to remain calm as Joni was so rattled by the conversation with Iva. Talking with my grandma was probably exactly what my mom needed for some reassurance. Grandma was always honest with her about Iva and knew one day she might reach out to her.

Dorothy picked up the phone, "Hello."

Joni was talking a mile a minute, "Mommy it's me, I don't know what to do, you have to help me; that woman, she called me just now, can you believe it? Why would she want me to go to some wedding, do you know anything about this ceremony?" Joni sniffled.

"Joni, slow down, what do you mean some woman, who called you that has you this upset?"

"IVA! My birth mother, she is inviting me to a wedding for one of my brothers, seriously, I can't do that, this has to be some kind of joke." Joni blurted as she was pacing in the hall.

"Honey calm down, when is the wedding?"

"It's in a couple of days; I think she said this Saturday and I have to work the hospital floors on Sunday, she also told me she already told one of my brothers, Jack I believe, and he is going to pick me up and take me there. I don't want to go. She said she is getting old and trying to see me before she gets too old. What do you think I should do?"

"As your mother, I understand why she is reaching out to you, it sounds like she just wants to meet you, maybe it would be a good idea for you to go and finally meet your birth mother and siblings."

"I know you might be right, but I just wish you and Daddy would go with me."

"I think this is something you need to do on your own if you decide to go and meet your birth mother; this doesn't change anything, and I hope you know that. You are still our little girl and always will be. Where is the wedding?"

Joni started to relax a bit, "I don't know she said she was going to call me back tomorrow."

Dorothy reassured her, "Honey, baby, again, I think you should talk to her tomorrow and try to keep an open mind. It is only one day, and you will finally have the opportunity to meet these people, maybe by attending this wedding you will find some peace or better yet closure, and you might even become friends with your brothers and sister. It may be a good thing."

"I suppose you may be right; I will wait for her to call tomorrow. I love you, and I will call you after I talk with her."

They hung up the phone; my mom was faced with a difficult decision; to go or not was the question. Reflecting on this challenging decision must have been hard for both my mother and grandparents. It does seem a bit risky to get in a car with a man you have never met before, but in this case, it was her biological brother. I do know my grandparents did not want her to regret passing up the opportunity to meet her biological family.

The next morning the phone rang. "Doyle," the dorm mother yelled, "you have a phone call; she says her name is Iva."

The minute she heard it was Iva, her heart began to beat faster, "All right, I'll be right there."

She strolled down the long hall and picked up the phone, "Hello Iva."

"I'm wondering if you have thought about my offer to come to your brother's wedding; oh, please say yes." Iva implored.

"I've thought about it and talked it over with my mother; I suppose I will go to the wedding." Joni begrudgingly responded.

"OH, I am so thrilled, I can't wait to wrap my arms around you, and for you to meet your brothers and sister, at last!" Iva said with such excitement in her voice. I'm sure she probably thought my mom was going to deny her request.

Joni interrupted, "You said my brother Jack would be picking me up, right?"

"Yes, I will call him right away and let him know, I will have him meet you in the lobby if that is okay with you," Iva replied with such joy in her voice.

"My daddy said he would make arrangements for me to fly

back right after the wedding so I can be back on Sunday, I have to work. I will just need someone to take me back to the airport after the ceremony if that is all right?"

"Of course, that is fine; Jack will make sure he gets you to the airport on time. Joni, I will see you at the wedding, and I am so happy you are coming. Jack is a tall man with curly black hair."

"All right, see you, bye." Joni quickly dialed her mom. "Mommy, I just got off the phone with Iva, I have decided to go. My brother Jack is going to pick me up here at the dorm, and Daddy is going to make arrangements for my flight to return in time for my Sunday shift, right?"

"Yes honey, he will get on that right away. I know this must be scary for you, but I do think it will help you to understand a little bit about your biological family. Again, it doesn't change anything, you are still our little girl, and your daddy and I love you so much." Dorothy tried to reassure her.

They hung up the phone, and now there was nothing but anticipation and fear of meeting all these strange people for the first time. The wedding was in Chambersburg, Pennsylvania; it was a three-hour drive from Pittsburgh. For the next several days, all she could think about was meeting one of her brothers for the first time, not to mention riding in a car with him for that long. It did seem a bit precarious; after all, she didn't know him, she had only seen pictures. What would we talk about, she wondered, and realized that this man, her brother Jack, was a complete stranger. She couldn't believe she had agreed to this whole affair. She wondered how this man felt about her; for heaven's sake, he was just finding out about her! She had butterflies in her stomach just thinking about meeting everyone for the first time.

The Family Meeting

Early Saturday morning, Joni got a call that she had a visitor waiting for her in the student lounge. Oh-My-Gosh, her heart began to palpitate faster than normal, her hands got clammy, and she thought she was seriously going to have an anxiety attack. She was about to meet her brother Jack for the first time! She was terrified. She thought to herself, "What will Jack think of me?" As she gathered herself and walked from her dorm to the front office, there he sat tapping his foot nervously on the floor, wiping the sweat from his forehead. I think he was around twenty years of age.

Mom continued to recount the story to me as if it were yesterday, describing what she wore, as she wanted to look her best and make certain everyone could take one look at her and recognize that she was well taken care of by the Doyles. She had on a beautiful scoop neck peasant dress with cap sleeves, a vibrant yellow and purple pansy design. Joni was quite tall, six feet to be exact, so she typically wore flats, and she picked the prettiest black shiny ballerina shoes to wear.

Jack was tall with dark curly hair, olive skin, and dark eyes, all traits like my mom. He was dressed very nicely in a black suit. When she moved closer to him and looked into his eyes, she could sense that he was as nervous as she was, his jaw clenched, eyes dancing in every direction, and sweat beading on his forehead. The anxiety curled in her stomach, blood was rushing to her cheeks, and her heart was beating so rapidly it began to fill her ears with white noise. She found herself chewing her lips fumbling for the words just to get the courage to introduce herself, "Is your name Jack?"

He replied with a shaky voice, "Yes, is your name Joan?"

Once they got the introductions out of the way, he led her to his car. It was a 1957 black Buick sedan with red interior. He was very polite as he opened the door for my mom. With some hesitation on her part; her feet seemed to be planted in the cement almost frozen, not moving, feeling slightly sick to her stomach. She told herself repeatedly in her head, "I can do this!"

Jack whirled his hand, motioning her, "Hurry along, we are running a little behind schedule, and I don't want to be late for our brother's wedding."

Hearing Jack reference other siblings seemed to make this situation, my mother's brother's nuptials, a reality. It just hit her like a ton of bricks that she was going to be meeting the people that were her family for the first time. When they were situated in the car, they were off. The first few minutes of the ride there was nothing but silence. As her heart began to beat even faster, it felt like it was going to jump out of her chest. All sorts of crazy notions flooded her head, questioning her decision in agreeing to go to this event. How could she go to a wedding to meet these strange people? Yes, it was her biological family, but the fact of the matter was that they were strangers.

Seeing Jack through her peripheral vision, his two hands were firmly gripped on the steering wheel, shoulders tense and his eyes sternly focused on the road. She wondered what he was thinking. Was he mad for not knowing all this time that he had another sister? Did he regret agreeing to Iva's demands in picking my mother up or was he just as uneasy as she was?

He drove like a crazy maniac, at speeds of 90 miles per hour, determined not to be late. She didn't care if they made it on time or not, but for Jack, she knew it was important. As they drove, he finally started to talk, just a little.

"So, you want to be a nurse, good for you."

"Yes, I do. My mom is a nurse, and I love helping people just like her. What about you, are you married?"

"Yes, I am, and her name is Thelma. She will be at the wedding. How long have you been in nurse's training?"

"I have been going to school for a year and a half; I am half way done."

"I just got out of the Army."

It was small talk, but she was getting to know her brother. It seemed the two of them finally started to relax a little.

"I met our grandfather when my parents tried to adopt me, that's when he told me Iva was not well and why she didn't show up."

As nervous as she was she did her best to stay upbeat. As they continued down the road chatting and getting to know one another, I think Jack sensed that my mom was happy with the Doyles. He envied her happiness and how her life had evolved.

"Iva wasn't always there for us, you were better off with the Doyles. For most of my childhood, my grandparents raised me as well as my brothers and sister."

In their conversation, Mom learned that Iva worked for Avon. I guess she was good, as she was one of their top salespersons. The downside is that she was never around for the children as she traveled a lot. I can't help wondering why Iva didn't find a career path that would have allowed her to be home with her kids more.

By now, it seemed clear to Mom that Iva put herself before others in her life, as the choices she made didn't make much sense. In fact, she learned probably more than she wanted to know about Iva on that long drive that day. Jack made it clear she was not a nurturing mother. That afternoon she had a new appreciation for her adoptive mother, who fostered her in so many ways.

She was astonished to find out from Jack that his siblings had no idea she existed. Iva was going to tell them just before the wedding. It seemed such a setup for disaster, and why would Iva put them all in this risky situation? Jack himself had only found out a few days ago, and I can only imagine the shock, as it was so much for them all to absorb. He had no idea that she was given away all those years ago.

Now she was anxious! What was going to happen at this wedding? Why did she agree to go? All she wanted to do was curl up in a quiet place and cry. Somehow, she held back the tears. As they drove, she decided that she had to make some sense of what she was about to encounter.

She glanced over at Jack. She thought to herself that he didn't look anything like her, except for the dark eyes. She was so hurt at this point, that deep down she did not want to resemble any of these people.

She began asking Jack more about the groom, "So the groom is a twin to Joyce, right?" He explained, "Yes he and Joyce are fraternal twins. Jerry had a heart condition and had heart surgery to correct it."

This piece of information was something for her to note, as she had no idea of any medical history in her family. As a nursing student, she was interested in finding out more. "Oh, said Joan, is he going to be all right?"

"Yes, he is fine, I suppose if it weren't for his condition, he might never have met his bride-to-be. She was his nurse when he first became ill."

Finally, as they were getting closer to the church, my mom became increasingly anxious, to the point where she was deeply regretting her decision. She felt like she was in a long, slow motion nightmare. More questions began to arise: Where would she sit? Would Iva insist on sitting with her? What if all her siblings instantly hated her?

"I have to hurry, Jack said. I'm a groomsman."

He pulled the Buick up to the curb in front of the steps like a racecar driver, so fast her body lurched forward when he stepped on the brake. Jack instantly pointed to a woman on the top of the church steps with a big hat. My mother looked up, and she was seeing Iva for the first time.

A tall man walked toward the car and opened it for her. He extended his hand to help Mom out of the car. "Joan, this is your older brother Jim," Jack said.

She gently tucked her dress and reached for his hand, "Hi Jim, thank you."

Her mind was racing with uncertainty. She was sure her siblings had similar mixed feelings. Jack and Jim walked her up what seemed like the stairs in the *Rocky* movie, where she was introduced to her birth mother. It was probably the most awkward moment of my mom's life where she attempted at first to avoid any eye contact. Iva was waiting for her on those church steps and alongside her was her sister.

Looking back, I find it crazy that my mom courageously could get out of the car that day and meet these strangers all by herself. She wished at the time her mother and father were there to help her get through the next several hours. Although she knew it would have been weird for them; therefore, she knew it was probably for the best that they didn't come. She did not want them to feel in any way insecure about meeting her biological family.

She did wish, however, that she had considered bringing Barbara. She would have been a great support, and she needed it that day. I honestly believe if Mom would have asked her to go with her that day, she certainly would have obliged.

Looking at Iva was like looking at herself in the mirror, she couldn't believe how much she resembled her. She also saw the strong family resemblance among her siblings, as much as she didn't want to admit that fact. Iva was tall, just like my mom. She had silver lush, thick overflowing locks of curls peeking out from her radiant hat she was wearing. Her hat reminded Mom of those that the ladies would wear to the Kentucky Derby.

She didn't have much of an extended conversation with anyone while at the wedding, except for Jack, and that conversation mainly occurred in the car when he was transporting her to the wedding. Immediately following the wedding, Jack and Iva drove her to the airport for her short flight home. While in the car, Iva tried to pin an orchid on Mom, which she did not want. To this day, she wondered why she was so insistent on pinning a flower on her, especially since she was leaving the wedding. Was it supposed to be some peace offering that would erase all her wrongdoings for giving her away; or maybe a token for making her attend a wedding that she was incredibly uncomfortable attending?

All she wanted to do was hurry up, board the plane, and forget that this awful day ever happened. Now, when looking back on Iva's gesture with the flower, I think it was her way of reaching out to her. I believe she was trying to make a connection with my mom. Although, I think at that time she was in no state of mind to be receptive on any level. In her eyes, the entire trip was one massive disaster.

She arrived late to the airport, and the worst thing that could go wrong went wrong, as Mom missed her scheduled flight. She was tremendously upset.

She began hysterically crying, "Oh no what am I going to do; I just have to get home to my mommy and daddy."

Jack did his best to console her, "It's going to be all right, let me think if there is another way . . . maybe the train."

She just felt so doomed and full of anxiety that she was going to have to stay overnight until the next morning, and that is the last thing in the world she wanted to do. She was also worried about her father, as he was supposed to pick her up at the airport. Suddenly she felt so alone; no familiar face to hold her, it was as if her whole world came crashing down. Jack quickly rushed her to the nearest train station. Fortunately, she could make the last train heading back to Pittsburgh that night.

When Joni arrived at the station, her father was waiting there to greet her with a big hug! She was ever so happy to see him. Missing her flight also meant missing her scheduled shift at the hospital. My mom was worried and concerned about how she was going to explain to the Director of Nursing why she did not show up for her shift. Once she arrived, she didn't waste any time to find the Director. She explained what had happened and the Director was understanding and sympathetic of the situation.

Happy to be home, was probably an understatement and she wondered to herself if she would ever see those people again. For my mom, she had indicated she didn't care one way or another if she did. She wanted her life to go back to the way it was. She realized now that as uncomfortable as the situation may have been for her, she did the right thing, as she probably always would have wondered "what if?"

She could finally say she met her birth mother and siblings. My grandmother put it very nicely, "Baby, you will have no regrets."

In response, my mom said, "Momma, I know you are right as you always are. I suppose I can say I won't have any remorse because that day made me appreciate you and Daddy even more."

The next morning her life continued, as it should. She went back to classes, and that stressful trip of meeting her birth mother and siblings became nothing but a distant memory—so she thought.

Chapter 8

Beloved Pen Pal

As a young girl growing up, my mother watched many of her friend's date young boys. She hardly dated while living with her mother and father. I remember her daddy being so protective of her. She was the epitome of "Daddy's little girl."

Oh, he was so worried that a boy might take advantage of his baby girl. He always reminded her, as he would say, "NO "hanky-panky" you hear, don't let a boy touch you or kiss you, it can only lead to bad things, and all boys are animals you hear!"

"Yes, Daddy, I get it, boys are animals." She chuckled.

Mom never really questioned him, but she did often wonder why he felt it was so horrible to let a boy kiss her. It rather reminds me of my dad being so strict with my sister and me. We had to wait until we were sixteen to date. Both of us were so anxious to go out on our first date, and for me, that seemed like an eternity. I was just a few weeks shy of turning sixteen, and boy oh boy, did I do some begging to go out with a boy I had such a crush on. Oh, he was a cutie!

With some convincing on my part, Dad finally agreed, but with that came a strict curfew. I can still picture my dad sitting in his chair scooted against the wall near the kitchen table. He would puff away on a cigarette anxiously awaiting my sister and me to get home. I made sure to always be home by my curfew because if I didn't, I was in for a severe tongue-lashing. He could not rest easy until his little girls arrived home in one piece tucked away in our beds. That is just how my mom's father was. I look back now and reflect on how endearing this was, but back then I despised being under such strict rules.

Back then, parents were reluctant to give "the" talk about the "Birds and the Bees." For Mom, that never happened. My mom was so naïve she remembers when a boy finally did kiss her for the first time she thought that she was pregnant. It wasn't until she attended nursing school she was educated about sex. She was also taught from a very young age that you remained a virgin until you met the man you were going to marry. In my mom's last year of school, Becky happened to be writing a man in the Marines.

Becky explained to her all about being a "Pen Pal." I must admit it is charming about putting pen to paper and taking the time actually to write a letter by hand. They got to know each other through their words. She remembered thinking to herself, how fascinating it would be if she were to meet the love of her life by writing letters.

She did have some concerns, as she wondered if the person she wrote to would lie and not be the person, they were portraying to be, but it seemed harmless. Shortly after the Vietnam War, my mom was introduced to a pen pal by the name of Ronald Webb; he was stationed at Camp Lejeune in North Carolina.

She was so excited when she received her first letter from him. His penmanship was good for a man, so she felt she was already off to a good start. Of course, the only other person she knew that wrote with such great skill was her father. His letter was concise but had one important fact. He described himself as being six feet two inches tall. That immediately grabbed her interest, since she stood six feet tall in her stocking feet, so she was eager to learn more about him.

After several weeks of my mother and father exchanging letters with one another, she received a photograph of my dad standing next to some of his fellow Marines. Seeing a picture of him for the first time made it seem so real to her; she thought he was so handsome. She so wanted to believe in love, and fairy tales that she did not for once believe that any of his letters or pictures could have been lies. Fortunately, for my mom, my dad was authentic; they fell in love simply through their letters. Soon after he sent a picture, she sent one of herself. She worried that her unusually tall frame would scare him off. Most men seemed to be threatened by Mom's height; my dad was not at all daunted; in fact, he was quite enamored by her stature.

They discovered they had quite a bit in common during the time they wrote back and forth to each other. My father's biological dad left his mother when he was very young; however, he was raised by a wonderful man his mother married, who also served as a strong male figure in Dad's life and whom he respected very much. He looked up to him for fatherly advice when he needed it.

My dad was a hard worker, which also delighted my mom. They wanted the same things in life, which were to settle down in a small town and start a family. It's hard to believe they never actually dated but only exchanged a few pictures and countless hours of drafting letters back and forth to one another. As both their hearts would grow fonder with each letter, my dad longed to meet my mom, but the distance between them was far. My dad did not have a car, nor did Mom.

By now, they had been writing letters for nearly eleven months, and Joni was close to finishing nurse's training. She had a break and was home visiting her parents. One evening she was quietly reading in her bedroom, and suddenly there was the buzzing of the ring tone. Ring, ring, ring—her Dad picked it up and hollered, "Joni, you have a phone call; it's some boy named Ron."

She jumped up like a jackrabbit and ran down the stairs to grab the phone from him.

She gasped and excitedly said, "Hello . . . HELLO."

"Hey, what are you doing right now? I'm downtown Pittsburgh and want to see you. Is there any way that you can come and meet me?"

Oh, My Gosh . . . my mom was ecstatic with joy! She couldn't believe he drove all that way. She skipped around her room like a giddy schoolgirl in puppy love. She was finally going to meet the tall, handsome Marine that she had been writing to all these months.

"How did you get here? You don't have a car, did you come by bus or train?"

"One of my friends has a car, and I talked him into driving me so we could finally meet each other."

"Oh . . . how sweet of him to volunteer to drive you all this way. I am so excited to see you."

"Yeah, we wanted to get away from the base for a few days, so I talked him into making the drive to Pittsburgh."

"What is your friend's name?"

"His name is Roy; I'm just grateful he agreed to bring me to meet you finally."

As exhilarated as my mom was to see my dad, the hard part now was telling her Daddy. "Okay, you know I want to see you, but I have to ask my dad. Don't worry though, I will convince him to let me go."

"Let's meet in the hotel lobby where we are staying, shall we say around 11:00 am tomorrow? We only have a two-day leave, and I have to head back to the base the following day."

"All right, I will see you tomorrow at 11:00 am sharp. Goodbye."

"Goodbye."

They hung up the phone and Mom was as nervous as a long-tailed cat in a room full of rocking chairs. She paced back and forth in her bedroom for a few minutes practicing aloud the words she would say to her dad. She realized no matter how much rehearsing she did, she needed to buck up, collect her thoughts, and tell him. As she opened her bedroom door to make her way to the kitchen, Frank's voice yelled out, "Joni, who was that on the phone?"

There was a pause as she made her way into the kitchen where he sat reading the newspaper alongside Grandma. She was glad her mom was present, as she knew if anyone had a soft heart, it would be her.

It was not a big dark secret that she was writing a Marine, but I don't think either one of them ever thought she would meet him. As like most father's, her daddy was overprotective, and Joni was his little girl that could do no wrong. She sat down at the kitchen table, her daddy in his chair and her mom in hers. Both sensed she was nervous and excited at the same time. "You are certainly happy about something. It wouldn't have anything to do with that phone call you just received?" Dorothy said.

Her voice shook a little as she responded, "Yes, as you both know, I have been writing a Marine for eleven months now." Joni enthusiastically replied.

Frank quickly said in a remarkable voice, "So let me guess, that boy on the phone is the Marine you have been writing?"

Joni replied in a soft voice, "Yes, Daddy. His name is Ron, and he and one of his friends drove all the way from North Carolina to see me." As she gazed into his keen eyes that attested to his quick wit, she begged, "Oh please tell me it is OK . . . he drove a long way to meet me."

He heaved a deep sigh, and looked over at Dorothy, "Mom, what do you think? Our little girl sounds like she might be smitten with this young Marine."

Dorothy replied, "I think it only right we let Joni go and meet him, but you are not going alone. You call your friend to go with you." Looking at Frank, "He can't be all that bad of a boy if he drove all this way to see our little girl."

With that, she quickly ran to snatch the phone to call her best friend, Barbara, "Barbara, you are never going to believe it, but remember the Marine I told you about that I have been writing? Well, he is in town and wants to meet me. He also came with a friend, and I can meet him only if I take you. Oh, please say you will go with me." Joni pleaded.

Barbara was in complete awe that Ron and Roy drove all those miles to see her. "Of course, I will go with you. Did he tell you what his friend looks like?" Barbara replied.

"He said he has blonde hair with blue eyes, and of course, he is a Marine! I am just so excited and happy that he made the trip. I just can't wait to meet him finally." Joni replied.

Barbara was laughing in excitement, "Well you can count me in, when are we leaving?" asked Barbara.

"I was hoping you could pick me up at around 10:30 am tomorrow, as he wants us to meet him in the lobby at 11:00 am. Does that work for you?"

"Yeah, no problem, I will see you in the morning. Make sure you look gorgeous! Goodbye!"

"Oh, I will . . . Bye!"

The next morning Barbara arrived at her home and rang Mom's doorbell exactly at 10:30 am as they discussed. Joni was so excited upon Barbara's arrival that she couldn't get to the door fast enough. Her dream of meeting this man was finally becoming a reality. She could barely think straight and chattered on and on anxiously while driving downtown.

Neither Ron nor his friend had much money, so the hotel they stayed at was not in the best part of town. When they finally arrived, Barbara parked the car in an underground parking garage.

When they got out of the car, Joni did a twirl for Barbara, "How do I look? I want to look beautiful for him, and I hope he likes me," Joni said.

"You look great and how do I look?"

"Beautiful, you look lovely. Ok, let's do this!"

Joni had on an A-line dress with a floral print with soft pastel colors, and short sleeves with a scoop neckline. It was topped off with a wide belt, and of course, you can't forget her flat Mary Jane shoes.

As she walked in the lobby, her heart was beating a mile a minute, thump, thump, thump . . . thump! She had a little clutch purse and was patting down her dress fretfully, ensuring herself that she looked ok. She scanned the room like a traveling spotlight, moving her eyes from face to face looking for a handsome Marine, hoping he would be in his uniform.

Ron spotted Joni first and walked directly towards her. He was six feet two inches in height, just as he said in his letters. Wow, she could hardly believe he was taller than she was. He was dressed in what they call their Charlie Uniform: green khaki trousers with a beige belt with a brass buckle, black spit shined shoes and a beige short-sleeved shirt. Ron looked so debonair dressed in his freshly pressed uniform; oh how it made Joni's heart go pitter-patter. His hair was brown with the usual high and tight Marine cut. His eyes were hazel with little flecks of gold and had eyelashes a girl would kill for, long luscious and curly. He introduced himself with a sweet devilish grin on his face. I think he thought he was going to get in my mom's pants that night, but not my mom! After all, she was taught you don't have sex until you get married. He soon found that out.

She stood there, practically paralyzed in her shoes as he walked closer to her: "Joni is that you?"

"Yes, I can't believe we are finally meeting."

He gave my mom a long tight embrace, almost to the point where she could hardly breathe. Ron was taken back by my mom's big smile, not only did she have beautiful lips, but he also loved her infectious laugh, which complimented her big grin.

While Barbara and Roy were getting more acquainted with each other, it seemed as though the world had frozen in time and they were the only two people in the room. To think my parents had fallen in love writing each other all those months ago, and that day they were finally meeting each other face-to-face. Oh, how she'd imagine meeting him, and there she stood in front of him gazing into those beautiful hazel eyes. It was an intense emotion for both of them as they hugged one another for what seemed like an eternity, as neither one of them wanted that feeling of being in each other's arms to end. They talked for several hours about childhood memories, passions, and their future.

"So how much longer will it take you to finish nurses training?"

"I am more than half way done with school, and you, how much longer until you get out of the Marines . . . and where will you go afterward?"

"Once I am out I plan to go back home. I am hoping to get a

job, and then get married. What are your plans when you get out of school?"

"I want to work in a hospital as a surgical nurse, just not sure where. I too hope to get married." At that moment, her heart was telling her wherever Ron was going to settle, that was where she wanted to be. It was getting late, and she and Barbara had to get home, not to mention Ron had to leave the next morning to report to his base.

There they were, still in the lobby off in a somewhat private spot all to themselves. I think my Dad was hoping to get my mom up to his hotel room, but that was so out of the question. They were getting closer to having to say goodbye to one another and in one of those rare moments in life, they knew they would be together again. The anticipation of kissing each other was building up. Joni had never actually experienced a passionate kiss, she thought when you kissed someone for the first time, it would be magical; at least that's what she dreamt. You either have chemistry or you don't despite the love you think you might feel, but Joni already felt like this was love. After all those months of writing him, she felt they had built an amazing connection. They would both sign their letters, "Love" . . . but they never actually said it to one another.

With his eyes locked on Joni, he took a step closer. She wasn't sure her heart ever pounded so fast in all her life. His palms were sweaty, and he was nervous as he noticed Joni's big beautiful black eyes. For a fleeting moment, he wondered how someone's eyes could be so dark, as you couldn't even see her pupils. He wanted to know everything about the girl standing in front of him and more than anything, I think my mom wanted to feel his lips on hers.

He leaned in closer, and finally, he pressed his lips against hers.

They began kissing, and he slowly inserted his tongue in Joni's mouth swirling it around. All sorts of thoughts were churning in my mom's head. Does she aggressively spin her tongue like a lizard or just follow his lead? He softly placed one of his hands on her shoulder and with the other gently ran his fingers through her hair. That one hand began to inch its way down her back towards her thigh slowly.

She felt a bit vulnerable at that moment, stopped him, and said, "I'm not comfortable with your hand there." Oh gosh, the look on his face; he was mortified. It's funny what goes through your mind when you are in the heat of the moment and what one another might be thinking. She was thinking all these hopes and dreams she had of meeting this man and falling in love, what if he only wanted to go all the way with her? Just at that moment, he politely pulled back and said,

"I'm sorry, the last thing I want to do is make you uncomfortable."

Her eyes began to well up, and she started to cry.

Ron stopped and said, "What's wrong, I didn't mean to upset you?"

She tearfully said, "Oh no, you did nothing wrong, I have been imagining kissing you and wanted it to be perfect, and it was everything I imagined."

"Then, why are you crying?"

"Because I don't want you to leave."

She sensed such a sigh of relief; he calmly reassured her they would see each other again. He leaned in and kissed her again. All that worrying about if perhaps her first kiss would satisfy him were dispelled; the kiss was more than electric. It sent shivers up and down her body. She couldn't believe that she was finally kissing him passionately for the first time, and it felt so right. For both, saying their goodbyes was heartbreaking. For goodness sake, they just met, and they were already being separated.

They held each other's hands as long as they could, then Ron asked, "Do you think it would be all right for me to come by your house to see you one last time before we leave in the morning?"

Turning on her heels, she blissfully said, "Yes . . . yes, of course!" Not realizing how hard it would be to say goodbye all over again.

Moving On

After that first visit, Ron drove to see Joni on several different occasions. Dorothy would make up a room for him on the third floor where he would sleep when he visited. Mom remained in the basement in her room, and you can bet Frank always slept with one eye open.

She finally graduated from nurses training in 1957, and all that was on my mom's mind was seeing my dad again. He also had just gotten out of the Marines, and he drove all night to see her. By this time, they had been writing and dating for nearly two years. She would have loved it if he would have planned a more elaborate romantic marriage proposal, but in his eyes, it was perfect. He did surprise her with a small but sweet engagement ring. It was a vintage traditional round diamond bridal set. I don't think it was even a quarter karat, but that was all he could afford at the time, and my mom was over the moon with excitement.

Before he presented the ring to her, he politely asked her father for his daughter's hand in marriage, and he, fortunately, got his blessings. Asking my grandfather's permission was like jumping off a cliff for him. As I recall her story, he had to pump himself up for that instant, but when that moment arrived, he felt like he was on the edge of a cliff looking down. When it was all over, he was so glad, but he knew he did the right thing by asking for my mom's hand in marriage. That was romantic enough for her.

They started to make plans about how she would make the big move to Danville, Illinois. Although she had just finished nurse's training, she was scheduled to take her required Boards exam of Registered Nursing. Though she took the test in the state of Pennsylvania, a passing grade granted her reciprocity in Illinois. She was confident she would pass, which she did.

They seemed to have it all planned, as he was to drive back to Danville, live with his parents and start looking for a job, and that he did! Once she completed her nursing boards, she would travel by train to Danville. Although my dad discussed where he was from, it didn't cross her mind what a small-town Danville was. In many of their correspondences, she never actually took the time to research his beloved tiny metropolis, which she would soon call home and the place where my mom would raise her children.

She was a city girl, raised in downtown Pittsburgh, Pennsylvania. She had envisioned what Danville might look like, as she spent so much time at the farm helping at the cottages in Evans City over the summers. That was as smallish as it got for her. Danville was a little country town located approximately 120 miles south of Chicago, 35 miles east of Champaign-Urbana and 90 miles west of Indianapolis, Indiana. The population today is around 33,000. As with many small country towns, and Danville was certainly no different, people speak with a southern drawl with a lot of "slang" or colloquialisms thrown in, which can throw off most any visitor. They would say stuff like "ya'all, pert-near, and dandy."

One knows you are in a small country town when you know all about the 4-H Club and on Friday's, if you want to find your friends, they could be found on Main Street cruising (where there is only one stop light if that) or at the nearby drive-up restaurant. Weekend excitement involved going to K-Mart, and your car was always filthy from the dirt back roads lined with cornfields.

This little town was all that my dad knew, outside of being in the military. He described it as a cute, quaint small town with charm and big city amenities, great parks, many antique stores, and most of all affordable housing. He also told her not to be surprised when she got off the train, as she would see chickens running around the train tracks. That should have been her first clue as to how small Danville was. The mere thought of my mom moving away from her parents terrified her; she was not sure if she could ever leave them. She knew if she wanted to make a life with my dad, she had to take a chance and follow him.

It was springtime; I believe sometime in May when she arranged to take the train. Her plan was to begin looking for work right away. It was after World War II, people were finally getting back to work, and the economy was starting to grow. It was evident that people were back to being able to pursue the American Dream of being gainfully employed and being able to afford to purchase a house. My mother and father were optimistic they would be able to obtain good jobs. She set her mind to it; she was going to move to Danville, Illinois. They didn't plan a big wedding ceremony with lots of friends and family. It seemed impossible with her family and friends in Pittsburgh, and his in Danville.

The day finally came to say goodbye to her mother and father. My grandparents were so sad at the thought of their daughter moving so far away. They did have such a wonderful relationship with my mom. For both my grandparents and mother it was flat-out heartbreaking. I know when saying goodbye to my mom when I moved to California, there was such an ache in my chest, an ache so dull and miserable that I was tempted to claw my heart out.

She was packed and ready to go to the train station; she was doing her best to be strong and stoic until she leaned in and gave her mother a hug. Tears began falling from their eyes, and she could not let go. Grandma loved my mom unconditionally and reassured her they would see each other often. Her father took my mom to the train station. I must wonder if that is why Grandma didn't go, as it would have been too hard to let go at the train station. On their way, he was being who he was, the best daddy ever giving her his fatherly advice.

"I loved you from the moment you came into our lives. I don't ever want you to forget that you hear! If things don't work out with that Marine, you can always come home, and I will personally drive to Illinois and get you." Frank demanded.

Choking back the tears, Joni said, "I know you will Daddy. I will miss you and mommy so much. Promise me you will write and call."

"I will and you know Mom will too. Now we better get going before you miss your train."

"Ok."

Grandpa parked the car and unloaded her luggage. He let out a grunt, "Joan Doyle, what in the world do you have in this luggage? It feels like you have everything but the kitchen sink in it."

"It's mostly my clothes remember . . . I am moving away and had to take all the things I will need."

"Just remember we can also mail you anything you might have forgotten. Promise me if there is anything you need, anything at all, you will let Mother and I know."

"Yes, of course, you know I will." However, she was too proud and wanted to show them she could make it on her own.

They finally approached the gate, and they were calling her train, "All aboard . . . All aboard." As she recounted the story, she so fondly remembers the sound of the rumbling on the tracks, the "Woo-woo" of the whistle and the conductor bellowing for them to board the train. The closer they got to the gate, the sounds were louder, almost deafening, in a mighty roar.

Gosh, this was it; she was leaving. Tears started to trickle down my mom's cheek, and her daddy wiped them with his finger, one by one, as they began to fall, reassuring her that everything was going to be okay. She hugged him, and he hugged her just as tight. I know he didn't want to let her go, but he knew he had to. His little girl was all grown up!

She finally boarded the train and quickly found a seat near the window. She pressed her cheek against the window with her hand waving goodbye and she uttered the words:

"I love you forever, bye-bye!"

As the train began to pull away, their eyes stayed with each other until they could no longer see one another.

Even though my mom was excited to see my dad, the tears continued to rush down her face. She did not take her eyes off the window. She drank in the scenery from the city landscape of all the wonders and strange things in downtown Pittsburgh. She realized that soon she would see a much different countryside. As she started to see the gritty industrial landscape fade away, she remembered all the beautiful sites Pittsburgh has to offer. The Fort Pit Museum, the shops, the cable cars, and where the three rivers meet is a remarkable sight. Goodbye Pittsburgh, Danville here I come!

Several hours into the train ride, they began to roll into the country. Joni was taking in the views of the countryside laced with beautiful wild flowers. The further south she got she started to see fields, fields, and many more fields of open lands freshly plowed. My mom wondered what might be planted in those areas. Many of the fields she passed that day were corn.

Joni noticed crops being far away from farmhouses and she was amazed at how big they were. Some went for miles. There were clotheslines near farmhouses with colorful apparel hung in the yards. Pastures with horses and cows roaming the meadow grazing the thick spring grass seemed to be the everyday norm.

As several hours passed by, she started to get tired and closed her sad eyes leaning her head on the window. Surprisingly, she dozed the rest of the way on the train, and the conductor announcing their arrival into Danville awakened her. When she awoke, she wiped her eyes with her fingers, staring out the window, where are the buildings—they seemed to have disappeared? What she saw was a vast amount of more open land.

Finally, when the train came to a screeching halt, she remembered the hissing noise the brakes made as they were pulling up to the train station. She could hardly wait to see my dad and wrap her arms around him. There he stood . . . she began to wave her hands, wondering if he could see her. He spotted her and started waving back. In the background, she saw the chickens just as Dad described—lots and lots of them roaming the railroad yard. The train couldn't stop fast enough for her to get off.

Wow, Ron was not kidding when he warned Mom of all those chicks. I suppose this was as free-range as it gets. Nowadays, we pay extra for free-range poultry and cage-free eggs. She was one of the first people off the train and heard the chickens clucking a soft peep as if they were welcoming her to Danville and all is well. As she began to collect her belongings, she realized she was about to start an entirely new life in this little town.

As she stepped off the train, full of expectations for the day ahead, my dad gently guided her down the steps. He grabbed her luggage, dropped it to the ground, and gave her the hug of a lifetime. It wasn't just a quick passing hug; it was something that touched her so profoundly it made her realize that this man loved and cared for her. This loving hug took away all the hurt and abandonment she felt on that long train ride after saying goodbye to her parents.

She expressed how happy she was to see him but couldn't help the undeniable tears emerging from the corners of her eyes. "I'm so glad to see you. I have missed you so much. You can't even imagine how hard it was for me to say goodbye to my parents. I miss them already . . . oh I do hope this ache in my heart goes away."

"I know it must have been hard for you to say goodbye to your family and friends, hell you are uprooting your life for me, and I am sure you are scared. I will try to do everything I can to reassure you that everything is going to be all right and besides, we can go and see your parents whenever you want." Ron proclaimed.

That hug and those words at that moment would forever change her life. She felt for the first time outside of living in her dorm, a real sense of independence along with contentment, wonderment, anticipation, and not just tears of sadness, but also tears of joy.

Chapter 9

The Special Day

Ron loaded up Joni's luggage, and their first stop would be to meet his parents. She was nervous, as she wanted to make a good first impression. Now that the ring was on her finger she was committed to becoming a member of the family, so if her in-laws didn't like her, she knew it would be an ongoing conflict in their relationship. My dad did his best to reassure her they were going to love her.

On their drive over, my mom was soaking up the small town's country charm. They arrived at his parent's house; my dad parked on the street in front of their house and pointed, "That's my house, the yellow one."

My dad was a real gentleman; he quickly got out of the car, ran over to the passenger side, and opened the door for her. She blushed as she got out and was happy to see they had a quaint little front porch. They walked through the front door; his parents were sitting on the couch watching television—they jumped to their feet to greet my mom.

"Mom, Dad, this is the girl I was telling you about, the one I am going to marry. Joni, this is my dad, Harvey and my mom, Edith."

Joni approached them and gave them a hug, "So nice to meet you, Ron has told me all about you both."

Harvey chuckled," All nice I hope!"

Laughing Joni responded, "Why yes, of course."

"You must be tired from that long train ride. Is there anything I can get you? We have cold ice-tea," Edith said.

"Some tea would be great if you already have it made. I was able to fall asleep on the train, so I'm not too tired." Joni replied.

Edith went into the kitchen and poured some ice-cold tea.

"So, Ron tells us that you are a nurse; you shouldn't have any trouble finding a job," Harvey said.

"Well I hope not; my plan is to apply at the Veterans Administration Hospital here in town. Before moving, I contacted them, and they need nurses."

"Well, I think you will be pleased with the apartment Ron found for the two of you. It's within walking distance of the VA," Edith said.

"I'm looking forward to getting settled in."

"Well, if you need anything at all, don't hesitate to ask us, we would like to help as much as we can," Harvey reassured her.

"Thank you; I will."

My dad was getting excited to show my mom the apartment he found. "We better get going I can't wait for you to see our apartment."

Joni stood up, with a broad smile on her face; she was elated to meet her future in-laws finally.

"Good luck," Edith and Harvey, said in unison, as they got in their car.

"Thanks again." Ron and Joni said, waving goodbye.

They took a deep breath and smiled at one another. "Okay, let's go see where you are going to be living as the future Mrs. Webb,"

Ron said. Mom's face lit up when she shared this piece of the story with me; it was evident by the expression on her face that it seemed like it was yesterday as she recalled her excitement. It was such a joy listening to her sense of happiness.

Making their way to the apartment located on Robinson Street, she noticed it wasn't too far from where Ron's house was. I think this put her mind at ease as she was going to be living there by herself until they were husband and wife.

When they arrived, Joni paused, and she looked at Ron and kissed him on the cheek.

"Thank you for doing all that you've done. I know I have been scared, as this has been a big change for me. You have gone out of your way to make me feel comfortable."

As they approached the front door, he fumbled to find the key in his pocket while Joni anxiously waited. He opened the door; it was small: the living room, bedroom, and kitchenette were combined into one single room. She stared down the tiny hallway, and there was a cute little bathroom with a tub. "How wonderful, it has a tub. I love to soak and relax after my long hours working the hospital floors."

"Yes, and a shower for me, personally I prefer taking showers."

It wasn't much, but it was theirs. Within a week, Joni secured a job. There were days she yearned for the bright lights of the city; it took some time to adjust to the slower paced lifestyle, but in time she managed.

Joni was often home sick, she longed for her mommy's cooking, and her heart ached for her familiar friends and the places she used to go. The excitement of when she first arrived in Danville was wearing off. Her nursing career, which she was so passionate about helped, as she met so many wonderful people and it did ease the transition. Of course, she had Ron's friends and his family who were all loving and supportive to her, which was very comforting. She met his twin sisters, Sandra and Linda, who would be at their wedding. She wrote her parents often, and they would talk on the phone weekly. It was challenging for Frank and Dorothy to visit, as running a seventeen-room boarding house took up much of their time. They, unfortunately, would not be able to be at her wedding. I know this broke her heart; however, her best friend Barbara was right by her side. They had always talked about being in each other's weddings and being each other's maid of honor. She was so excited for Barbara's arrival.

It seemed that Joni endured her long-distance romance with my dad better than being apart from her best friend. It was hard on her being so far apart from her as she was the one person who knew her better than anyone. Barbara knew her every secret, the one person my mom would call in the middle of the night with a crisis.

The reunion finally arrived; she and my dad were picking Barbara up at the tiny airport in Danville. Amazing, this was Barbara's first airplane ride, she didn't know what to expect. She took a jet from Pittsburgh to Chicago and from there a small puddle jumper into Danville. She was missing my mom as well and was excited to reunite with her.

Clear the road, other drivers, because my mom was on a mission to pick her up. It was as if she was trying to rip a hole in time and space to get there as fast as possible. She and my dad finally arrived, and her aircraft was minutes from landing. She found herself pacing until she heard the woman announce over the intercom, "Flight coming in from Chicago has landed."

"Woohoo—she's here, she's here!" Joni said as she was jumping up and down with excitement. It was a wet dark evening as it had been raining before her arrival. Barbara was deplaning, and as she carefully walked down the steps, she looked around, and she got a cold shiver down her spine.

Joni was waving her hands in the air, "Over here . . . over here!"

The glow of the light from the front of the airplane barely illuminated the next few feet of the pitch-black darkness as she crept along the dank wet pavement.

"Oh, my gosh . . . where in the hell did Ron move you to? I feel like I just got off a plane in the middle of nowhere, and it's so dark outside, I can barely see you!" Barbara shrieked.

"Ha-ha." They laughed.

Joni ran and hugged her tight, "Finally, you are here. Did you get a haircut? Is that a new dress? I can hardly wait for you to see my new little apartment," Joni blustered.

Her words spilled out in the incorrect order like hot lava, as nothing made sense because she was so excited to see her best friend.

"We have so much to do in such little time before my wedding," Joni said.

"Well . . . I don't want you to worry your pretty little head. I am here now, we will get everything done, and your magical day will be perfect!"

"Did you get my bridal veil done as you promised?"

"Of course, I did, it's in my suitcase. I just have a few final touches."

"Oh, I can't wait to see it, what does it look like?"

"Well, the length of the veil falls just below your elbows because I didn't want to make it too long since you are wearing a waltz length ball gown. The design of the halo has a band of seed pearls and sequins sewn on by hand. I know it will be a perfect match to your wedding dress. You are going to be such a beautiful bride walking down the aisle to meet Ron."

Left to right: Linda, Sandra, Barbara, Joni, Ron, Warren, and Ron's Uncle and Cousin

"Ha-ha, I am sure I will, and besides, we don't have time for you to redo it since my wedding is tomorrow."

It was almost as if my dad was just along for the ride as their driver. They chitter chattered back and forth all the way to the apartment. Once they arrived, a relative calm settled over their initial hysteria and they couldn't wait to get in their pajamas so they could get into the gritty details of everything that had happened over the course of the time they had been separated.

Ron carried in Barbara's luggage, and he couldn't leave fast enough so they could get their pajama party going. When they finally were settled in, they began finalizing the last-minute details of her wedding. The thing that had been missing in her life snapped back into place as if she finally completed a puzzle. No matter what life throws at you or how long you are apart, seeing your best friend again is like picking up where you left off all those months ago. There was a couch and a double bed in their humble little abode. Barbara slept on the sofa and my mom in her bed. They were tucked warmly under the covers and trying to wind down, as they were just so excited to see one another they talked into the midnight hour.

Boom! A loud noise sounded . . . beep, beep, and beep. It was the alarm clock. They jumped out of bed and wobbled one by one into the bathroom. The sun peeked in the windows, and my mom opened the curtains to let in the vibrant sun rays. It was a beautiful day to get ready for a wedding.

It was August 15, 1957, and their wedding ceremony was to be held in the afternoon. Mom and Barbara started getting ready in the apartment, and they would meet the others at the chapel. They didn't have a lot of money, so they kept everything small and intimate.

"Okay, okay Joni, you need to breathe, can you do that for me?" Barbara asked.

Fifteen minutes before the ceremony, Mom was as nervous as most brides tend to be. The last time she felt this nervous was when she met Ron for the first time. Joni was beautiful, wearing a waltz length gown of white Dacron Villon with a scooped neckline outlined in pearls and sequins.

She also carried a prayer book topped with an orchid surrounded with a tufted net, and green and white satin streamers.

"I can't breathe. I just wish my mommy and daddy were here to help calm me down."

Sandra and Linda, her sisters-in-law to be, were her other two bridesmaids. They were dressed in matching waltz length gowns of blue, and their headpieces were the same color. They carried colonial bouquets of pink and white chrysanthemums.

"Joni, it's almost that time." They said.

"What do you mean, how much time do I have left? Barbara, you must get my veil pinned in my hair now. Hurry!"

"Look," Barbara said, "calm down we have plenty of time people are still getting seated." She shook her head in worry, "You still have to get your headpiece on."

Barbara wore a beautiful pink lace and taffeta waltz length dress. She also wore a matching headpiece she made and carried a colonial bouquet with blue and white chrysanthemums.

"Ok, it's on! It's about to start. I see Ron waiting at the end of the aisle, and he looks just as nervous as you do. We have to line up and get ready to go." Barbara said.

The church looked stunning, decorated for a day to remember. The altar was lined with beautiful lit candles along with baskets of white gladiolas and chrysanthemums. The pews were marked with greenery and white bows. There was a prelude presented as the bridesmaids made their way down the aisle accompanied by a soloist, where she sang "Always and Because."

The sweet little flower girl wore a lavender satin dress. She lined the path with white rose petals and the music started. Ron's uncle escorted Joni down the aisle since her daddy could not be there. Ron's best friend Warren was the best man, and his two other groomsmen were his uncle and cousin.

Finally, the reverend came out and asked everyone to stand. It was my mom's turn, and every eye would be on her. As she took a few steps, Ron's uncle greeted her. He escorted her down the aisle, which seemed longer than before. She was sad that it wasn't her daddy walking her down the aisle, but he became her strength to forge on. The guests looked up at the bride, smiling, waving, and no one made a sound as the wedding march presided.

My dad's future wife looked up ahead, and she saw him; her future husband, the love of her life standing so tall with his shoulders back, his hands folded, and his eyes fixed on my beautiful mother. Mom being the sap she was swore she wasn't going to cry, but she couldn't hold back the happy tears that filled her eyes. She could have sworn she saw a tear emerge in my dad's eyes.

She made it to the end of the aisle, and Ron's uncle gave her a hug and presented her to my dad. As a couple, my parents stood in front of the reverend. Barbara gave her the thumbs up that she needed to get on with the nuptials.

Wow, was this happening? Joni was soon to be Mrs. Webb. The reverend seated the few guests that were there. He looked at my dad and then my mom, "Dearly beloved," he began, "we are gathered here today to join this man and woman in holy matrimony." He said the standard wedding vow speech and my parents exchanged their vows; tears were rolling down from her eyes. Warren handed my dad the rings, Joni placed Ron's ring on his finger first then he gently slid her ring on her finger.

After they had exchanged rings, they performed the traditional candle lighting ceremony symbolizing their marriage. They turned, towards the guests, and the reverend introduced them as Mr. and Mrs. Ronald Webb. As they left the church, everyone stood and applauded for the newlyweds. Blessed were my mother and father to have found such a profound love for one another.

They were beyond hungry as neither one of them had eaten anything all day. The guests followed behind them as they made their way to the reception. It was held at Harrison Park Clubhouse. The bridal table was adorned with a three-tier cake decorated with pink and white flowers. There were also beautiful bouquet arrangements placed on every table. When the happy couple arrived, they were announced, and they had their first dance. There was applause from the guests as they danced to a soft melody. They circled each other, and their gaze remained locked into one another's eyes.

It was a night to remember, and everyone who attended the reception had so much fun. My parents left immediately following the reception, as they were expected back in Pittsburgh because my grandma planned a picnic party for them. They traveled all night along with Barbara in the car with them. My mom insisted Barbara ride back to Pittsburgh with them in the same car. To this day, she questioned her decision, as she felt they should have been alone on their wedding night, but my mom would not hear of it, and my dad kindly obliged. Funny thing is she sat in the front seat most of the way to Pittsburgh.

Barbara knew how scared my mom was about having sex for the first time. She was supportive and tried to reassure her that everything would be all right. So much anticipation of the thought of finally being able to be sexual with the one she loved was exciting but at the same time daunting.

Nowadays we have the Internet, so it leaves nothing to the imagination. If someone wants to know about sex, you just Google it. My mom was worried it was going to be painful. As a student nurse, she had to give bed baths to men and may have accidentally seen their penis, but she had never touched one. At first glance, it was somewhat intimidating to her to think that thing would somehow fit inside of her.

She had heard so many stories of the different sizes and variations of what new husbands might look like but never had she seen one completely erect. She realized that much of her fear was psychological, but the whole act just all seemed so awkward.

As my mom recounted the story, she remembers Dad driving faster than normal, and she was sure he was anxious to consummate the marriage. Ugh, was her thought. Seems silly to me but since sex was not talked about back then, it must have been nerve-racking for her. It's a shame it was not taught in school because her parents never talked about sex. It almost seemed like it was a bad word.

It was late that evening, and they finally arrived in Pittsburgh. It was so surreal for her to see the big city lights again. They dropped Barbara at her home first before they made their way downtown to 514 N. Neville Street. She loved downtown Pittsburgh, crossing over the bridge gazing upon the lit-up skyline with the lights flickering and glowing, and the reflection on the waters of the Allegheny and Monongahela Rivers was breathtaking.

They finally arrived at the house. Grandma and Grandpa were waiting up for them. Grandma always greeted her loved ones so endearingly, "Oh kiddies, I'm so glad you made it safe and sound!"

She knew they had been driving all day, and they were tired, but remember not too tired, as my dad was overly excited to finally be able to sleep in the same bed with my mom. Grandma had a room all ready for them on the third floor. It was one of the nicest rooms in the boarding house. She even placed fresh flowers and towels in their room. As they began their way up the stairs, her heart began to flutter like the wings of a hummingbird!

OK . . . my mom thought to herself, "How bad can this be; it seems that having sex is a part of intimacy . . . right!"

My dad was more than nervous as you can imagine. He wished they would have stopped on the way from Danville to Pittsburgh and stayed in a hotel. Mom wouldn't, as her excuse was getting Barbara home, even though she was more than willing to get her own room.

Mom spent hours shopping for a beautiful wedding dress at Kaufmann's downtown Pittsburgh, and Barbara reminded her to make sure she bought something cute and soft to wear in the bedroom. After all, it was for her honeymoon night. She didn't wear anything sexy to bed, so this was something that didn't come easy for her. It looked like a slip with thin spaghetti straps, no special shaping, and the length hit right around her upper thigh. It did not have any bra structuring, and it was pink. I'm not sure why she picked pink; I guess it was because they were the colors she had in the wedding. There was beautiful lace trim around the top as well as the bottom. It was fashioned with a sense of modesty, but for Mom, it held a sense of sex appeal.

The newlyweds finally reached the third floor and entered the room. It was apparent that there was sexual tension between the two of them. They became quiet. She began searching for her nighty, and while they were getting settled, she said, "I have to freshen up a bit," and she went into the bathroom.

Joni slipped into her new pink nighty, took a deep breath, and whispered to herself, "I can do this!" She looked herself over in the mirror and slowly opened the door swiftly tiptoeing across the floor like a ballerina slithering between the sheets. Ron was already in bed with the covers over his body.

The room was dimly lit, their eyes locked and they began kissing. The lingerie enhanced Joni's charm and femininity. Ron took the lead, pulled her in closer, and whispered, "I love you."

"I love you, too," she said reaching for his hand.

He held her hand to reassure her. He gently slipped his tongue into her mouth, and their lips were locked. She was breathing as though he sucked the life from her. They fought their way to the edge of the bed, holding each other tightly.

He watched her blush as his hands found the straps of her

nighty to pull it off. Joni gently grabbed Ron's hand and raised his fingers touching her lips, "I'm so nervous." she said.

"Don't be," as he nibbled a bit on her ears. He ran his fingers through her thick curly hair.

Lie back and enjoy, she thought. I believe she finally managed to suppress her embarrassment and was beginning to relax and like it. Joni wrapped her legs around Ron hanging on for dear life. Trembling and moaning, she melted against the sheets, her legs still locked around his hips. She was somewhat intimidated making minimal sounds. She didn't know what to expect. It seemed that all the awkwardness had been swept away. It was gentle, and it didn't hurt. It was so worth the wait.

She laid her head against the curve of his shoulder, wrapped her hand around his arm, and breathed in the smell of his skin. "I know you will keep me safe, she whispered, thank you for being so patient with me."

He sighed with relief and tilted his head, so his forehead rested against hers. She let go then and let the sands of sleep engulf her.

The next morning, they were awakened by the smell of Grandma cooking her bacon and eggs. She rolled over and gently tapped her husband on his shoulder. "Wake up sleepy head, my mom is fixing breakfast, and you don't want to miss that." Ron, still half-asleep, grabbed his clothes and jumped into the shower. Joni followed and got herself freshened up. They raced to the kitchen to sit down to eat breakfast.

Joni was thankful they were able to drive to Pittsburgh and spend some time with her parents after the wedding in Danville since they couldn't attend their nuptials. Grandma did such a good job planning a nice picnic for them. She added special touches that made the farm sparkle as though it were intended for a couple of newlyweds. Grandma made up picnic baskets filled with goodies.

There were some table's already in place on the grounds, so they pulled enough of them together to ensure there was enough seating for everyone. Grandma picked flowers from her garden the day before; they added such a whimsical touch. Grandma made her delicious fried chicken, potato salad, and baked beans.

"Welcome to the family," Frank said, coming over to give Ron a handshake. "How's it going? I hope you like the party?"

Ron nodded. "Yes sir, very much so. I am grateful that you and Dorothy planned this as it means the world to Joni."

Frank slapped Ron on the back. "Stop with the sir crap." He chuckled. "You can loosen up; this isn't the military, don't be so stiff. I just want you to take care of my baby girl, that's all I ask."

Ron smiled, "I will . . . I feel like the luckiest man on earth!"

He met so many of Joni's relatives that day he was having trouble keeping track. His eyes were on my mom all day and hers on him.

Several hours passed and everyone started to disappear after saying his or her goodbyes. There were empty paper plates and cups lying on the ground that needed to be picked up. As they began cleaning up the mess, Joni noticed Ron making his way towards her. She smiled, and he kissed her on the cheek, "You have a great family. I am on cloud nine as I am married to the girl of my dreams, so forgive me as I don't want this moment to end."

Joni nodded, happily. "Thank you for bringing me home to see my parents, it means so much to me!"

He blinked at her, "Of course, I'm glad we made the trip."

My grandparents couldn't have planned a more perfect day for them. As she told me the story, it was as if it was etched in her memory bank forever. I suppose it was the simplicity of the celebration; not nearly the fuss that we think of today when planning a wedding. I know it meant so much to my grandparents that they could share a slice of their happiness that day since they couldn't be at their wedding ceremony. The next morning, they had to get back on the road, as they had to get back to their jobs. My dad had just started a new job in Danville at a printing company.

Frank and Dorothy packed them up some food to take on the road. They gave them a hug and said: "Thanks for bringing our little girl home to see us. I hope the next time you visit you can stay longer."

Joni began to tear up, "We will, won't we Ron?"

Ron smiled, "Say no more, of course we will."

"Promise."

"Joni, of course, we will!" She smiled, ran, and gave her parents another giant hug while saying, "Goodbye, Mom, goodbye, Dad," as they got in their car.

Her mom and dad were everything to her, and she was off to make a life of her own with her new husband. Their goodbyes saddened my mom, and it was very difficult for her. Who would sing and make her laugh like her daddy? Whom would she ask for advice, as she so often did with her mom? She wanted to get back out of the car and chase after them, but she knew she would have to face the inevitable goodbye all over again. She lowered her head in sadness and Ron reassured her that he was that person. She looked back as they pulled away, knowing she would see them again. The environment looked so peaceful and calm; something she had not noticed before. She could see her parents waving goodbye next to her house one last time. With her right hand, she waved to them, hoping that they would see each other sooner than later.

Chapter 10

Life in Danville

Slowly they began to settle into their new life in Danville. It wasn't long after that they found the studio apartment too cramped for the both of them, so they began looking for a bigger place. Since their funds were tight, her parents decided they wanted to help establish them in a new home. They gave them $1,000 to rent a small house located on McReynolds Street; the house looked like a little dollhouse, tiny and sweet. It was white with black shutters; the lawn was impeccably landscaped with flowers lining the front with a detached garage. It had two bedrooms and one bathroom. What she liked is there was a cute little park across the street.

What's mine is yours, and what's yours is mine was the mindset my parents agreed on in their marriage. They decided to have the same checking and savings account. My mom was responsible for managing all the bills; it worked out perfect for them.

My dad started his career as a printer apprentice while Mom continued to work at the V.A. for a short time until she was offered a better position in Danville's community hospital. She had strived to be a surgical nurse and was so excited to make this change; it was her dream job as a nurse.

She was slowly adjusting to her new way of life as a wife and a newly-wed when she would share some great news with my father. It was a cold February morning, and she was getting ready for work. She sipped her cup of coffee and paused while she couldn't remember the last time she had her period. She went to work and realized that she could actually be pregnant.

"Pregnant, I can't be pregnant—we are not ready for a baby." She muttered to herself.

There weren't any home pregnancy tests back in the 1950s. In those days, a urine sample was collected and sent off to a lab, and you didn't get your results within minutes, it was days. The anticipation of waiting seemed like a lifetime. She spent the rest of her day worrying and wondering how she would tell my father. Mom was fortunate she worked at a hospital so she could be tested that day. It wasn't as if they did not plan to have children; they were just going to wait until they each were more settled into their new life as husband and wife. She didn't want a baby right then, but she thought to herself, either way, she would be okay with whatever the results might be. Sometimes life doesn't always work out the way you plan it.

Several days passed and she got a phone call from her doctor that she was indeed pregnant. She felt somewhat ambivalent, and then she quickly realized she was going to have a baby. She wasn't sure how she was going to tell my dad, but she knew he would welcome the news and be overjoyed to be a father. So many thoughts were racing through her head; she viewed parenthood as something that would happen eventually but not anytime soon. She wasn't sure if she was ready to be a mother, as the concept of raising a child hadn't entered her mind as of yet.

When she arrived home from work, my dad was already there; she had the results neatly tucked inside her purse. Thirty minutes had passed; she was contemplating how she would break the news to him. Finally, she reached into her purse, handed him the piece of paper with the results, his eyebrows rose as he looked down at the piece of paper, "Uh, what is this?" he asked, a bit dumbfounded.

"Just open it." You could hear the nervousness in her voice. My mom sat on the couch with her arms crossed as he opened it. She wasn't sure how he would react.

He opened the envelope, and his eyes lingered on the paper. "Holy cow! Does this mean what I think it means?" His voice trailed off in a soft but shocked tone.

"Yes, I'm pregnant . . ."

"I'm going to be a dad—are you sure?" He looked up at her and smiled.

"Yes, I am convinced, we are going to be parents."

The nervousness had left her voice and joyfulness was creeping in. Ron jumped to his feet, grabbed her, and wrapped his arms around her kissing her all over her face with joy.

"Do you know how far along you are?"

"I'm not sure, but according to my calculations, the baby should be born sometime in October."

"We have to tell our parents; they will be so excited to be grandparents."

"Yes, I know, I can't wait to tell Mom and Dad."

All of the worry and nervousness was gone, and pure joy filled the room and their hearts, they were overwhelmed and excited, it was a bowl of mixed feelings. The news hit them both like a ton of bricks, as they knew their lives would change drastically with a baby in the picture.

Although they just moved to their quaint tiny house on McReynolds, that was not where they wanted to raise a child.

They knew this life-altering change would be beautiful and challenging, but at the same time, they were not prepared to move.

"We have to find a bigger house, and soon," Ron insisted.

"We just moved here, how can we just up and move, where will we go?" Joni cried big wet tears.

"You know, it's going to be all right, I am going to build us a house like I always promised, that is where we will raise our family."

"I guess . . ." The hesitation in her voice was evident.

"We will figure it out, one day at a time." He assured her as he held his bride close.

Although they were not ready, they figured out how to accept this new turn in their life. She was missing her parents terribly and couldn't wait to tell them; after all, this was tremendous news. She called her parents the next morning to give them the news. "Mom, is Daddy at home?"

"Yes, he is, is everything all right?"

"Guess what?" The enthusiasm in her voice was more than evident.

"What, what is going on, you're making me nervous."

"There is no other way to tell you this as we are on the phone, but you and Daddy are going to be grandparents; I'm pregnant!"

There was screaming on the other end of the phone: "Frank, get in here! Joni is on the phone; she's going to have a baby."

He quickly grabbed the phone from Dorothy and gushed, "My little girl is having a baby?"

"Yes Daddy, I got the results yesterday, the baby will be here sometime in October."

"Mom and I are so happy for you and Ron; we will have to come and see you when the baby is born."

"Oh, that would be so wonderful; I can't wait to see both of you, I miss you so much!"

"All right, I am going to hand the phone to your mother; I love you and make sure you keep us posted on your progress, good-bye for now."

He was still hooting and hollering with joy as he handed over the phone.

"Joni, I am so excited for you and Ron. You will be a great mommy. I just know it."

"Well, I hope so, I am still adjusting to the idea of becoming a mother, but I suppose that is normal. I have some mixed feelings, but Ron and I are happy."

"All right baby, I won't keep you as I know you have to go to work. I love you, and we will talk soon."

"Yes, I will keep you and Daddy up-to-date. Goodbye, I love you too."

When the conversation ended, Joni felt a sense of relief; still, she wasn't sure how others would react to the news. They were newly married and were working hard to make a better life for themselves, and now there were going to be three of them. She was hesitant and scared about what others might think, but she decided to announce her pregnancy to the world. She quickly decided she would work right up until her due date.

Just as the newly-weds were getting used to their schedules, they had to get accustomed to the idea of a newborn. It was challenging as they worked opposite shifts. My mom worked first shift and my dad second. They didn't see much of each other Monday through Friday, although they did their best to make time for one another. To compound the issue of being pregnant, Mom was feeling incredibly homesick; she was about four to five months into her pregnancy, and her hormones were running a bit high; Dad decided to take her mind off missing her family and friends. It was early spring, that is when the morel mushrooms start to pop up.

He packed up the car with some bags, a walking stick, and off they went to the nearby woods to hunt down these delicious treasures. Mushroom hunting was a new experience for Joni.

"How will I know when I find the right mushroom, and how do you know if what I am picking is safe?" She was so puzzled.

He began to laugh, "I'll show you; they look like sponges." My father explained, Morel mushrooms have a unique earthy flavor that simply can't be topped everyone should experience them once in their lifetime. Most people fry them up and eat them. "They sprout up under leaves and brush, almost like they are playing 'hide-and-seek.'"

"What? You will just have to show me." Joni was still confused.

Walking through the forest surrounded by the spring air, and smelling the moist dirt in search of magic, was so much fun for my dad. Mom, on the other hand, was a rookie at best but when she finally got the hang of it, she too couldn't wait to join the 'shroomers' hunting expedition each year. The bag helped with carrying them, and the walking stick would help to uncover the brush and leaves that would often cover them.

"Over here!" Ron yelled, "I found one, come look!"

Joni quickly ran over to get a glimpse of what the enchanted morel looked like. "Well look at that, it looks like little honeycombs all over the fungi. Are you sure you can eat that?"

"Of course, there is nothing like a crispy, mouth-watering delicacy like these mushrooms."

"How do you cook them?"

"You cut them in half, soak them in salt water, egg, and flour and fry them up in some butter. Mm-mm good!" His mouth was watering in anticipation.

Who would have thought stumbling through the forest would be so much fun, was my mom's first thought? The grasses they stepped on were somewhat mushy beneath their feet because of recent rainfall. She was in awe of the majestic trees that covered her like a canopy and the sun peeking through, illuminating the lush green sward. If that isn't enough to get you excited about tromping through the woods, there is the sound of the happily chirping birds and the rustling noise of animals running in the brush; the smell of the forest was so fresh you could almost taste the wildflowers rising in the crisp air.

Trekking through the woods was the best stress relief for both of them; it was just what the doctor ordered for my mom's homesickness. I remember my dad once telling me when he took me hunting for mushrooms, "If we want to fill our bags up we have to be patient." There were times when we would go out, and we might not find any, but when we hit the jackpot, we sometimes came home with several pounds.

They were successful in finding enough that day to make a meal out of them. It was a process but so worth it once she took her first bite.

"Okay, remember the first thing we have to do is put them in a salty bowl of water."

"Yes, but why can't we just rinse them in a strainer?"

"Trust me you use the salt for a reason. In about five minutes you will see exactly why."

"OH MY LORD! Bugs are crawling from the holes! How will we know that we got them all out, I am NOT going to eat insects, especially while I am pregnant. They better not make me sick."

"They will not make you sick, but that's why we have to soak the mushrooms in the salt so that the tiny little bugs will creep out of the crevices; besides, a little microbe won't hurt you and what the salt doesn't kill, the hot butter will." He was kind of chuckling now.

As they listened to Johnny Cash on the radio, they danced around in the kitchen while frying the mushrooms. My dad was a big fan of Mr. Cash; he used to listen to him endlessly. The first batch was done; Dad grabbed one and dangled it over my mother's mouth, taunting her. He then patted her tummy. "Not only are you going to be amazed at how yummy these mushrooms are so is our sweet baby. Okay, are you ready? Fried morels are divine cooking at its best!"

He slipped the mushroom in her mouth, and she began chomping and swallowing enthusiastically. It was heavenly! "Oh yes, you are right, I would never have guessed wild mushrooms to be so flavorful."

This was exactly what my dad was expecting to hear. "Lip-smacking right!"

My dad was not much of a cook; in fact, he rarely did any food preparation. Mom was the chef in the family. Happily, for my mom, that day was special to her as he shared one of his favorite pastimes and they could spend some time in the kitchen together. Mom decided to whip up some of my grandma's famous fried chicken to pair with the mushrooms, but my mom didn't realize how filling the mushrooms were on their own.

Grandma once shared with her that a way to a man's heart is through his stomach. Mom certainly paid attention in the kitchen when her mother would show her the basics. My mom won over my dad's affection with her cooking in no time. They sat down at the kitchen table, and dinner was served every night.

"Thanks for taking me mushroom hunting, this has been a terrific day."

"You're welcome. Can I get you some water?"

"Sure, thank you."

Ron grabbed a tumbler, cracked some ice in a glass, and went to the kitchen sink to fill up her glass. "I'd like to know why there is hardly any water coming out of this faucet?" He queried.

"That just started, it just barely comes out, and it seems we hardly have any water pressure. I don't know what's going on, but ever since last night, the water pressure dropped."

"Did you call the landlord?"

"No, not yet but I will get on it first thing in the morning." As they sat down at the dinner table, there was odd silence; Joni wasn't sure if it was a good thing or not. The dinner was so good, they were speechless, not to mention how hungry they were and Mom, of course, was eating for two. She grew up where dinner time was an important event for the family. It was a time when after a busy day, they would gather around the table and reconnect with one another. Eating supper as a family is a tradition that was carried down throughout their marriage, and continues now with my family. I cherish those moments where the whole family can enjoy a meal together. Conversations were spontaneous and unpredictable. They finished their dinner, and they were stuffed.

Joni had on a snug pair of pants that hugged her growing belly; she giggled as she patted her baby bump. "I ate too much since I've been pregnant, all I can think about is eating; I feel fat."

"Oh, stop it, you're not fat, besides you are eating for two."

"Oh Ron, she cooed, I enjoyed myself today. Thank you; I needed this so much, it took my mind off of how homesick I am and how much I miss my parents."

They each took a moment to relax and wind down before they did the dishes. My mom was a bit of a neat freak, and the kitchen was calling her name. My dad not so much, he was perfectly content just relaxing with the newspaper, sipping his water. He would have been fine with just leaving the dishes in the sink to pile up.

"That was such a wonderful dinner; it's a good thing those mushrooms only come once a year!" Joni laughed.

My dad was pleased she enjoyed them and agreed. "Yes, I have been hunting them since I was a little boy. It will be a tradition we pass along to our kids."

"Okay, I am going to tackle these dishes. I'll wash, how about you dry, and it will be so much quicker." He hopped up to help. They began cleaning up the kitchen; it didn't take very long with the two of them working together.

Welcoming Danny Boy

With a child on the way, they knew now, more than ever, living on McReynolds Street was temporary. It was time to make a move towards their dream house. Both of them wanted the American Dream - to build a house with a white picket fence. Thank goodness for my grandparents, as they helped them once again with a down payment for a piece of land that my dad picked for the house he would build for his family. It was a Saturday morning, and he couldn't wait to show my mom the setting of where he imagined their ranch style home.

"Joni today is a big day, I can't wait for you to see the land I found to build our new home."

"Okay, let's go, I can't wait to see it either." Joni was so excited she could hardly wait.

They jumped into the car, full of anticipation and excitement. They headed out to the property located at the North end of Danville, off Denmark Road and Gravat Road. It was a beautiful drive as they passed over the bridge of Lake Vermilion. There were miles of open land all around them. Still it was only about ten miles from their quaint rental on McReynolds, but it seemed far.

Finally, they arrived, and Dad pulled into a dirt driveway with several plots of land that appeared to be divided up. They got out of the car, and he grabbed Joni's hand, walking her to the center of the property that looked directly at a vast cornfield.

"Look, this is where we are going to build our home; I picture a ranch style home with a big beautiful picture window facing the cornfield. What do you think?"

"This is all ours? I don't know what to say; it's beautiful. How much of this land is ours?"

"We have an acre; we will have plenty of room to build a nice house with a yard for a family, and dogs."

She couldn't help but join in his enthusiasm. "A dog, we are getting a dog?"

"Well eventually; you like dogs, don't you?"

"Of course, I love dogs; I'm just thinking about building the house first."

"I want it to be a home where we can raise a family and have lots of pets."

"Me too, I can't wait for you to break ground and start construction."

It was certainly a process as my dad was determined to build the family home himself along with his dad and some of his friends. I consider this adventure ambitious, especially when they were expecting their first child in just a matter of months. I can't even imagine taking on the construction of building a house not having any experience. Surprisingly, my dad was more than eager to take on this endeavor.

They agreed on a ranch style home, three bedrooms, one bath, and a family room neighboring the kitchen, a basement, and two-car-garage. At the time, they didn't realize it would be wise to build more than one bathroom. It's not as if they didn't have the desire to create more than one bathroom; I think it came down to cost, especially since they wanted to put in hardwood floors. In the 1950's, it was common to build homes with only one bathroom, something that would not be considered for a house that size today. Looking back, I think we were a close family after living in that house, and while two lavatories would have been nice, it was easier to keep just one clean.

There were many times when Mom doubted that he could get the house done, as he worked forty hours a week and would work on the house endlessly in his spare time. For my parents, it was remarkable to see their home being built from the ground up.

It was October 11, 1958, and all was quiet in their house, it was the middle of the night, long before sunrise. Joni held onto her stomach and tapped Ron on the shoulder while he was sleeping. "I think the baby is coming."

"What! Are you sure?" He woke up from a dead sleep, and now wide-awake. He was in a state of disbelief; although he imagined the baby coming, he couldn't believe the moment was now.

"Yes, I think my water broke, and I am having pain in my belly, we should go to the hospital." She was very uncomfortable and was having a difficult time standing.

"I'll get your bag to the car." Ron rushed to retrieve the pre-packed hospital bag and put it in the back seat of the car and came back for Joni. While Joni was getting dressed, Ron quickly gathered her things to take to the hospital. "Just calm down, and I will help get you to the car."

"All right, hurry!" Joni was obviously in a lot of pain.

The couple arrived at the hospital; they were lucky the emergency room wasn't very busy; they took my mom to a room right away. As they were wheeling her into her room, a gush of water came out of her body, causing my dad to shriek.

It's getting close, the nurse said. I am calling the doctor. The medical staff quickly got my mom into bed. My dad was by her side. Back then the father was not allowed to be in the delivery room when the baby was about to be born, but Dad stayed as long as they would let him.

"Goodness, try to breathe Joni, I know it hurts; try to rest between each contraction."

Dad could feel her pain but could do nothing about it except try to soothe her.

Joni was trying to relax as best she could in between her contractions. The pain was evident on her face as she lay in bed. Joni screeched in pain with every contraction; she was ready for this baby to come out as the contractions continued to wear her down.

The doctor finally arrived. His name was L.W. Tanner. It was time for my dad to leave the room, and he was swiftly escorted to the waiting room.

"It's time," Dr. Tanner said. "Joni, I'm going to need you to push."

She listened - she pushed, and pushed, long and hard; unfortunately, the baby didn't budge. An hour had passed, and she was finally making some progress. Dr. Tanner could finally see the head. To my mom, and as she often reminded my sister and me of not having any pain medicine, she said the pain resembled a watermelon being pushed through a tiny hole. It was as if she had gone to hell and back and there was no end in sight. Joni just wanted it to be over.

"How much longer?" Joni screamed, "I don't think I can push anymore."

"Your baby is almost here; you just need to give me one more big push. Ready, Joni on the count of three, PUSH!"

She pushed with all her might. She wanted that baby out, right here, right now! The child slowly began to work its way out. That big long push finally got the job done. Half the baby exited Joni's body, and Dr. Tanner could pull the baby out the rest of the way. Immediately after the doctor cut the cord, the baby began to cry. "It's a boy! You have a beautiful, healthy little boy!" Dr. Tanner said.

"It's a boy! Can I see him?" Joni cried with big happy, joyous tears.

"Yes, in a few minutes, the nurse needs to clean him up."

"Someone has to get Ron. Please, can he come back now?" She implored.

"Yes, just hang tight. We are going to get you and your baby settled, and I will get your husband and give him the news."

"Oh wonderful, thank you."

A few minutes had passed, and the nurse placed the baby in my mom's arms. Joni cooed tones sweetly while gazing at her new bundle of joy with so much happiness; he was perfect. His tiny fingers curled up around her pinky. His eyes were more brilliant than she could have imagined they would be. He was only a few

Frank holding Danny and Dorothy

minutes old, and within that moment, he began to cry the sweetest tears. She couldn't take her eyes off him.

Ron finally made his way to their room to get a glimpse of his new baby boy. He could not stop looking at him, ensuring that he had ten fingers and toes; he was such a proud father. He was relieved and amazed at my mom as she just delivered this precious bundle of joy. He too couldn't take his eyes off him. Sniffing his newborn, he thought to himself, "There's nothing like the fresh, slightly sweet, and immensely satisfying scent of a newborn baby."

"Joni," the doctor said, coming in with a huge smile, "what have you and Ron decided to name your beautiful baby boy?"

Joni sat up in her bed and nodded, looking at my dad, "Ron and I decided on the name Daniel Doyle Webb, after her father, Daniel Francis Doyle.

They had tears of joy coming out of their eyes. Danny Boy had finally arrived. The Doyle name has always been paramount to my mother, and she was more than proud to be able to name her son after her dad. A side note, I too chose to carry the Doyle name with my son, Devin Doyle. I know he is proud to continue their legacy.

The Webb family arrived home with their new son, Danny. My grandparents had never been to Danville, but as my grandfather promised, he and Dorothy would make the long-awaited trip to visit their first-born grandson. Grandparents usually have the benefit of interacting with their grandchildren whenever they have the time; however, for my grandparents, it was a challenge, as they lived so far away. I think my mom was worried her parents would not be able to form a bond with Danny due to the distance between them. Before the advent of technology we have today, it was more difficult to keep in touch; however, they managed to adore Danny from afar.

Joni and Danny enjoying a hot summer day—Neville House backyard

It was a day my mom long anticipated; the arrival of her parents to meet Danny. They made the very long drive from Pittsburgh. Joni was patiently waiting, peering out the window every five minutes anticipating the arrival of her parents. She was cradling her baby boy in her arms when suddenly she heard tires crunching on the rocks approaching the driveway. Joni swiftly jumped to her feet. She peeked out of the window and saw the car pull up. "Ron, come quick Mom and Dad are here, you have to help them in the house."

Joni yelled with excitement. "Okay!" He dashed out of the family room. "I'll be right there." Just as he was reaching for the doorknob, he heard a knock at the door - tap, tap, tap.

"Joni, Ron, it's Grandma and Grandpa." They muttered through the door.

He opened the door, and they fussed over the sight of seeing their baby girl holding their grandson. Big smiles emerged from

Ron in awe of his preious Danny boy

their faces as this particular gift was about to be handed to them. "Oh my goodness . . ." as Joni placed Danny in her mother's arms, "Grandma is so excited to meet you finally." She was in awe of her grandson. Dorothy stared into her grandson's face with tears in her eyes.

"I didn't think it possible to love someone as much as I love you Joni, but I do; he is so precious." Grandma Dorothy sat on the couch and soaked up the bliss of holding her beloved grandson. Grandpa Frank was gaga as he gawked at the gorgeous sight of this image of Dorothy embracing Danny. It didn't take long before he announced, "Ok, you're hogging all the cuddle time, it's my turn."

Grandma Dorothy passed him to Grandpa Frank, and he

began the infamous baby talk. "Oh . . . look at you. You are the most beautiful baby in all of the lands."

"I so wish we lived closer so we could spend more time with him." Grandma Doyle said.

"I know you do, and I too would love it if you were nearby; however, I know your home is in Pittsburgh, and we will visit as much as we can."

"If your dad and I lived close by we would be able to babysit." Grandma Dorothy said.

"I would certainly love that, but I know it is impossible. We will send lots of pictures and make sure that we call you weekly with updates."

They were thrilled to have that precious time to spend with not only Danny but my mom as well. They gave their unconditional love, kindness, comfort, and support in abundance. They may not have had the luxury of being physically present, but they did not skip a beat when it came to keeping in touch. I can recall growing up that Grandma never missed an opportunity to send my sister and me a card for our birthdays and all the other important holidays. We never doubted Grandma Dorothy's love for us, as she always made us feel special.

Chapter 11

Building Their Dream Home

They lived on McReynolds approximately two years until they had the roof finished where they could finally move in. Before that, I am sure they had no idea of how challenging it would be coping with the mess, especially now more than ever, as they were also caring for a baby. After several years of living through the chaos and wondering if there was an end in sight, it certainly made them appreciate their home so much more.

At last, Mr. and Mrs. Webb and Danny arrived; their home was full of promise. Cardboard boxes were sprawled all over the house next to the bare walls. Their priority was to get Danny's room set up. Mom loved decorating and proved she could spruce up a room with a can of paint or wallpaper. For my mom, it was also important to incorporate items and designs that would stimulate the baby's development; however, they were also on a tight budget. Her primary concern was only making sure his room looked and felt like it was a little boy's room, so she painted the room a soft blue.

The house was the right size, and my mother would eventually make it feel homey with her whimsical flair for decorating. The windows were not large, more like the size, in old country homes. The living room floor was hardwood, but it seemed that back then, shag carpeting was far more fashionable. The kitchen and family room floor was polished linoleum, which was easy to maintain. The laminate was installed to withstand the abuse that children and dogs typically dish out. Unlike the seventeen-room boarding house where my mother was accustomed to the accents of dark teak and walnut wood, she knew that she wanted to decorate each room with brighter colors and a sense of authenticity.

The basement was constructed of cinderblocks, making its walls quite thick. My father would make this part of the house his workshop where he set up his workbench, while Mother would have enough space for a laundry room as well. It seemed like the perfect area to store belongings, but what they didn't account for was the water seeping in from the earth when there were heavy rainfalls. I can recall living in the house when we spent our time squeegeeing the basement floor after heavy precipitations.

Living out in the country meant they had to dig a well for water and a septic tank. As my mom recounted the story, I never really realized just how challenging it could be. What they thought would be a good spot turned out to be dry. After shoveling multiple holes about fifteen feet deep, they found no water. My mom was getting discouraged, as she had no idea what the process was in excavating a well. "Do any of you even know what you are doing?" Joni blustered.

Dad solicited several men to help him with the project. Anyone who knew my mom certainly knew that she was a woman of conviction and not much for any monkey business. I think they were all trying to figure it out, and they continued to make errors based on their judgment about just where to start. It seemed they broke up the earth for hours and still no H_2O.

They laughed at my mom and pointed to yet another place to hollow out another pit. "This is the spot; we will soon have water!" Ron exclaimed.

They began again, this time about twenty feet, still no wet stuff. They were starting to get tired, as they had been at this most of the day. I'm not sure how far down you have to dig, but at some point, your hope is to find the source. One would think you would make sure there was water on the property before you build a house. My father was sure that this would not be a problem. As day turned into night, they realized they had to pack it up and start over fresh in the morning. They had very few neighbors, which were scattered over several acres. Fortunately, their closest friends allowed them to use their garden hoses for water until their well was complete.

The alarm went off, and Ron, still half-asleep, jumped up out of bed. Joni got up and made her way into the kitchen to brew a pot of coffee. The smell of freshly brewed coffee is all it took for my dad to get his motor going. "I hope you have better luck today." Joni was sincere.

"Yeah, you and me both."

Once he had his "cup of Joe" and breakfast, he was ready to face the world. Today was the day they were going to hit the water. He was determined! He quickly dialed up his helpers, and within minutes, they arrived with their shovels in hand. They began digging another hole; they probably dug down about twenty feet. One of the neighbors came over to witness their hard work. As he stood watching, he asked, "How many holes have ya'all dug?"

"Oh, hell, since yesterday I've lost count."

"Well, may I suggest you all might want to stay in one place and dig a lot deeper; you will eventually hit the water."

They all looked up; having dug many different holes, they realized he might be onto something because the only water that was gushing out was their sweat. They dug deeper and deeper, and before you knew it, they found abundant water.

"Woo hoo! Joni, come look we finally have water!"

My mom ran outside and was never so thrilled to see water gushing out of the ground.

Finally moving into their home was truly the American Dream. My dad was so proud of his accomplishments; looking back at all the hard work in building their home without contractors is admirable.

The house was down the road from dairy farmers whereas a little girl I remember getting fresh milk from time to time. When one would look out the picture window, there was a view of a vast cornfield. On one side of the house each summer, my family, along with my neighbors, used to plant a large vegetable garden. My mom and some of the neighbors would all work the garden together, as well as my sister and me. I suppose it was an excellent way to bond with family and friends because we would all pitch in digging, hoeing, weeding, and watering. It was a daily chore keeping up with a full vegetable garden. If there is one thing I miss, it is fresh organic vegetables. We planted sweet corn, green beans, peas, carrots, radishes, cucumbers, squash, melon, tomatoes, lettuce, and peppers. We always tried to plant more than we needed so that we could can our vegetables for the winter months.

Everyone in this tight-knit neighborhood looked out for one another. It was fun to be able to count on your neighbors in times of need. One particular family friend, the Browns, were considered our second family. Their hearts were always in the right place, as they looked out for our family throughout the years, and we would do the same for them. We lived on a one-acre lot, which may not seem like much land when you live in a rural area, but when you have to push mow the yard, it is a lot of yard to cover. Our neighbor saw my dad walking behind the mower in the hot, humid sun, and much to his surprise, they showed up

House Ron built on Gravat Rd., Danville, Illinois

with their riding tractor, and what would typically take several hours to cut the grass, only took a half hour.

In the winter, Danville used to get quite a bit of snow, and my parents didn't have a snow blower, but what they did have was a long driveway. There were times when their car was covered with a foot of snow, and it seemed there was no end in sight to get out. Shovels were all they had to manage all the snow. It would take hours, and the neighbors could see the constant struggling.

"Hey, do you want some help?"

"Thank you, but I think I'm okay." My father never wanted to be an imposition.

Looking at my father struggling they knew he needed help, "You sure?"

He paused for a second, looked at all the snow that still needed to be removed, and before he could say anything they were shoveling with their tractor; the Browns were great neighbors.

We were fortunate, as the Brown's continued to remove the

snow from our driveway every time we got a snowstorm. As for the grass, they helped my dad until my parents could afford a riding mower.

Unexpected Loss

It was a cold November morning, and the phone rang way before the sun was up. Joni jumped to grab the telephone, and she wondered who could be calling so early.

"Hello!" Joni mumbled, as she was half-asleep.

Dorothy was sobbing, "Oh baby, it's your mother, your daddy had a stroke. He's in the hospital . . . he is stable for now, but the doctors don't think he is going to survive."

Joni collapsed to the floor, as she was stricken with fear that she would not make it to him in time to kiss him goodbye, "Oh my gosh, he just has to hang on until I get there. I will get on the next flight out. I will contact Barbara, and she will pick me up. Please tell Daddy I am coming, and I love him."

Joni hung up the phone and quickly woke up Ron; she was barely able to keep her composure, and she began to shake Ron, out of fear until he woke up "Ron, wake up, wake up . . . Daddy had a stroke. I have to go be with him, and you need to take me to the airport."

"What? I will go with you."

"Oh Ron, as much as I want you there you have to stay and take care of Danny. A hospital is no place for a baby."

Joni frantically threw some of her clothes in a suitcase while Ron called the neighbors to watch Danny. The drive to the airport seemed like a lifetime, as she was so worried that she wouldn't make it in time to kiss her father on the forehead one last time.

Joni arrived at the airport in a panic, realizing this would probably be the last time she would see her daddy alive. Mom pushed her way through the airport until she finally made it to her gate. There were just a few minutes left before they began boarding. The waiting was so difficult; she wanted on the plane and no delay in taking off. She sat and held her head in both of her hands, and cried. All my mom could think about was losing her beloved father.

"Miss, are you all right?" Asked the gentleman who was sitting next to her.

Joni wiped the tears from her eyes, "No, my daddy has had a stroke, and I am trying to get to him before he dies, it doesn't sound like he is going to make it."

"I am so sorry to hear of your father's illness; I will say a prayer for you and your family in this difficult time. Try to stay positive that you will make it to your father in time."

They boarded the plane, and she buckled herself tightly around her waist. Although this was a relatively short flight, this was going to be the longest hour she had ever spent on a plane. She didn't want to talk to anyone and was hoping she would sit next to someone who was quiet so not to bring attention to herself as she held back the tears. She closed her eyes and held her hands, praying that she would get to her father in time.

Finally, the plane landed, but the wait to deplane seemed like it was taking a lifetime. Joni slowly began to edge her way off, and as she walked through the walkway, she held her head high scanning the room for Barbara. Barbara was standing near the gate where she waved and yelled: "Joni, over here."

Joni dropped her suitcase, threw her arms around Barbara, and said, "We have to hurry!"

"I don't want you to fret; I will get you there, I am here for you; whatever you need you understand?"

"Yes, I don't know what I would ever do without you, you are a true friend. I love you!"

They arrived at the hospital; Barbara dropped her off in the front; Joni ran inside, some nurses were standing near the receptionist desk. They saw the tears in my mom's eyes and asked if they could help her. They directed her to her father's room. As she was walking towards his room, she stared at the room numbers on the doors, counting them down until she made it to her daddy's room. Her head was hanging low with sadness as she entered the room. Grandma was sitting by his side holding his hand. She made it; she threw her purse on the floor and hugged her mother. The world just stopped for a moment as she held her mother close, both sobbing knowing it was just a matter of time.

"What are the doctors saying?"

"Your father had a stroke, and right now he is being kept alive on a ventilator."

"What happened, how did this happen?"

"He got up to go to the bathroom, lost his balance and fell. I heard a thump and ran to find him on the floor. He grabbed his head, squinting his eyes in pain. He wasn't responding to me, and I knew it couldn't be good. I called the paramedics, and they rushed him to the hospital."

The doctor told my grandma the news that it was indeed a stroke. She was in disbelief as if she was already at his funeral. She didn't know how she was going to go on without him. It was bad!

Barbara finally parked the car and made her way to the room to find them both holding Frank's hands. She took a deep breath, slowly walked towards Dorothy, and gave her a hug.

"I'm so sorry; as I told Joni, let me know if there is anything I can do."

"Thank you, Barbara, I feel like this is a nightmare, and I am going to wake up, and everything will be all right."

"We have to decide whether to take him off life support. I know Daddy would not want to be kept alive with a bunch of machines."

He was hooked up to so many apparatuses, a heart rate device that kept beeping regularly along with the hissing sound of the respirator. They were mainly keeping him on life support waiting for my mother to get to him. They now had to make the unbearable decision on when to withdraw him off the ventilator understanding that death was inevitable. Letting go of a loved one is probably by far the hardest judgment call that anyone might have to face in his or her lifetime.

Life is so unpredictable, and a life lesson I learned when saying goodbye now to both my mother and father is respecting their final wishes. My sister and I thanked them for always being there for us. My mom believed that her father was thankful that he was put on life support so he could say goodbye before taking his last breath. Knowing that my mom was there with my grandma, his beloved wife Dorothy, in the days ahead I know gave him solace and peace to be with the Lord.

The time had finally come to take Frank off life support. It is such a difficult decision for anyone to have to make, but my grandma and mother knew he would not want to just lie in a bed hooked up to a bunch of machines. He had already been diagnosed, without a doubt, to have a condition that was not survivable. Removing life support, was at this point the kindest and most humane thing to do for him. The doctor agreed that even if Frank had awakened, he'd have been a vegetable and permanently immobilized. Being nurses, my mom and grandma were understanding of his condition and realized that he had no chance of recovery. They knew the machines were keeping him alive.

"Please, can you make sure he doesn't suffer? I just don't want to see him in any pain." Joni was anguished over losing her father.

"Of course, we will make sure he is as comfortable as possible."

Both agreed that Grandpa would not want either one of them to linger over him in hopes he might have a slim chance of regaining consciousness; however, how do you just "pull the plug" on someone you love so dearly? His body was still warm; they were holding his hand, and his face was still there for them to kiss him goodbye. They leaned in, and whispered, "I love you!" The doctor was present, and they finally gave the order for him to pull the plug. Both their hearts were screaming; somehow find a way to keep him alive! I don't think anyone is ever ready to make such a horrific decision.

The doctor gently removed the tube and reminded them that it could be minutes, hours, days, or weeks. Deciding to end his life was inconceivable. However, the doctor reassured them that it would not be painful. His respirations slowly dissipated, and he was gone within minutes. He passed away on November 27, 1960.

I think when my grandfather finally passed away, although it was a shock to my mother and grandmother, they knew it was the right decision. Frank was a resilient and independent man; they knew if they were to bring him back somehow, he would have been terribly mad at them.

Joni stayed with my grandma to help her get through this difficult time. As per Frank's wishes, he did not want a funeral with people walking by his casket saying goodbye; he believed this to be nothing more than a burden to my grandma and mom. They abided by his wishes and did not have the usual traditional service. Grandma had him buried at St. John's Lutheran Church in Connoquenessing, Pennsylvania.

Mom was apprehensive to leave my grandma. "You know," my

grandmother said with sadness, "I don't know what I would do without all your love and support." She raised her arms to hug Joni. "You're the only one that I can count on who understands what I am going through at this difficult time. I love you with all my heart, but it's time for you to go home and be with your family."

"Mother, that's what daughters are for, and I wouldn't want to be anywhere else but here with you!"

Dorothy smiled, hugging her tightly and said, "I won't ever forget what you have done for me. Your father would be so proud of you. Now you have to get going, and I will see you soon."

As Dorothy was trying to get my mom off and home safely, Joni's eyes began to water. She started to walk away, and suddenly turned around and gave her one last hug.

"I'll see you in the summer when we all come up to visit you. I love you, and I will call you when I get home."

Grandma wiped her tears away, "Joni, I am going to be all right. Now get going. I love you more than you will ever know." I know Grandma wanted to chase after Mom and have her stay, but she knew my mom needed to get back home; her baby now had a family that needed her. Barbara also was moving to Danville because my parents had introduced her to the man she would marry. Knowing she would soon be living near my mother was comforting to her.

Chapter 12

Twins & Tragedy

The one value Grandmother held above all others was thankfulness; she instilled that in Joni, and it was a principle value to my father as well. My mother said I needed to appreciate everything I have as when she was a little girl, their family had very little. However, the feeling of gratitude for my mother was valued, as she did feel blessed to have been put in the arms of the Doyles all those years ago. After losing her beloved father, she realized now, more than ever, just how fortunate she was to have had such a wonderful daddy!

Joni was fast approaching her 25th birthday, and they were slowly settling into being parents to Danny when they decided it was time to plan for another child. They began their quest the summer of 1961. It was only a matter of months, and she got pregnant sometime in the fall. Most people have time to prepare for twins, but in my mom's case, she did not. In the 1960's it was just not standard practice to have an ultra sound, except under extreme circumstances, or if the parents had a lot of money or fantastic insurance; none of which did my parents have.

It wasn't until the 1980s when ultrasounds became a standard practice. My parents lived on a tight budget, and she didn't even remember being offered an ultrasound. One would think in the case of a woman's belly doubling in size as opposed to a single baby the doctor may have considered the possibility of twins, and perhaps even mentioned it to her. Since Mom was six feet tall, she could carry the children in a manner that didn't cause alarm. She only gained a total of 26 pounds when pregnant, and she carried all the weight in her belly. When she was recounting her experience, it amazed me that during her nine months of pregnancy, Mom had no idea she was carrying twins; she went into labor around 4:00 am on June 2. She felt some cramping and back pain, which prompted her to peel her big belly out of bed slowly. As soon as she stood up, she felt a warm gush of what she thought was urine like most women do when their water breaks.

She quickly realized her water had broke and abruptly woke Ron up; he was swift on his feet to help Mom get her things gathered to go to the hospital. They called ahead to let them know they were on their way, but before they headed off, a nurse asked Joni a few questions. "How far apart are your contractions . . . are you timing them?"

She responded, "No . . . I have not been timing them, but my water broke."

"You and your baby better get to the hospital!"

She was getting anxious, "We are on our way. Please call my doctor, L.W. Tanner. I don't want any other doctor to deliver my baby, so you have to call him."

"When is your baby due?" Mom's due date was June 7, which was close to my dad's birthday, June 9. I think he was hoping she would have the baby on his birthday. Dad scrambled so much to get Mom ready to go they almost forgot about Danny, who was fast asleep in his crib. He was running around the house looking for his keys while

Mom screamed, "Ron we have to call our neighbors to come and watch Danny."

"Oh, hell, I can't believe we almost forgot about our son. It's not like this is our first time."

He frantically got in touch with the neighbors, and as soon as they arrived, they were off to the hospital. On the way, Joni's contractions were getting much stronger. She remembers Ron driving the speed limit.

She yelled, "Drive faster!"

He began whisking by the few cars that were on the road. He slowed the car down in front of the emergency room exit. Across the way, he saw a security guard standing near the entrance.

"Hey, Ron yelled, I need some help over here. My wife is about to have a baby."

The security guard ran inside and got a wheelchair for her. Joni was no stranger to the hospital staff as she worked there. They wasted no time getting her situated in a room where they began monitoring her contractions. L.W. promptly showed up and examined her, and much to her surprise she was already dilated three to four centimeters. The contractions were getting much worse, and she was feeling the urge to push, but it wasn't time yet.

Ron stood beside her holding her hand and wiping her forehead with a cold cloth. It was getting closer, and he was escorted out of the room where he would meet up with Auntie Barb. Ron looked to Joni, "I love you; I will see you and our little one soon."

The labor pain seemed a bit different than what she remembered when she gave birth to Danny; this time was by far much worse. She had heard of babies just popping out after only a few hours of labor and was so hoping that would happen. She ignored the clock and relied on the nurses to check on her to assure her everything was going just fine. With each contraction, the pain got harsher. "Oh gosh, is this baby ever coming out? I don't think I can take this pain much more."

"You're doing great Joni; just try to focus on the beautiful new baby you are about to meet, and you will not even remember the pain once he or she arrives."

Now, I'm not so sure that is entirely accurate, as I was in labor for thirty-two hours with my first child, and I have not forgotten the pain! It was getting close, and before she knew it, she was fully dilated. She was more than ready to start pushing. She pushed, and her baby arrived. Oh, but wait, hold on to your horses.

"Holy Cow!" Dr. Tanner yelled, "You are having two, not one!"

"What, how is that possible?" Joni screamed.

Twin A came out headfirst, and within seconds, Joni was told, "It's a girl!"

Apparently, the umbilical cord was wrapped around her, and Joni questioned L.W.,

"Are you sure it's a girl?"

"Yes Joni, I'm sure! You have a beautiful little girl." L.W. said.

He knew they were in for a bit of a struggle with twin B, as she was lodged in the birth canal breach. With much bearing down and the help of the medical staff, twin B finally came out twenty-one minutes later.

You typically do not hear of twins being born so far apart. Twin A was born at 11:45 am weighing in at 6-pounds-5¾ ounces, and twin B was 7-pounds 2-ounces born at 12:06 pm. Mom used to joke that if she had had them around the midnight hour, they would have been born on two different days. It is hard to believe that my mom carried my sister and I full term . . . what a blessing!

My dad was in the waiting room oblivious to the fact that he was about to be a father to twins. Fortunately, Mom's dearest friend accompanied him. While she was holding her two beautiful baby girls, Joni was bursting with joy, "I just had twins! Ron is going to be so surprised when he realizes there are two babies, not one!"

Dr. Tanner was stunned, "Joni, I am going to get him so he can meet his daughters."

"OK." While lying on the gurney, she turned her head from right to left staring at the babies in her arms.

Dr. Tanner entered the waiting room where Dad and Barbara were eagerly waiting. "Ron, Joni and the babies are doing quite well." Dr. Tanner said.

"Did you say, babies? You mean baby right!" Ron said.

"Ron, you have beautiful twin girls." Dr. Tanner confirmed.

As he stood there while Dr. Tanner delivered the news, everything suddenly got blurry. He felt nauseous, dizzy, and light-headed. What just happened, he thought to himself? Barbara was trying to talk to him, but she sounded so far away.

"Ron, are you okay, you look like you just saw a ghost!"

"I think I am going to faint," Ron muttered.

"Sit down and let me get you a drink of water," Barbara said.

He sat down and took a sip. For the moment, the room stopped spinning, and he began to feel normal. I think he was in shock realizing that he was taking not one, but two babies home. Dad and Barbara went to my mom. She was being wheeled out of the delivery room where she laid peacefully on the gurney holding their twin daughters. For the moment, they were referred to as twin A and twin B. They were not prepared with two names. They had tossed a few names around, but neither one of them had anything solidified before their birth.

Candy (twin A-right) & Connie (twin B-left)

They were going to wait until after the baby was born to decide; however, in this case, it was two!

The nurse carefully handed him twin A first and then twin B. Barbara was in complete awe!

"They are just beautiful Joni," Barbara said.

My dad, still in shock, looked down at his two baby girls, looked up at Barbara, and said, "I'm glad you think they are beautiful, but these babies are ugly!"

Now, we all know that newborns, in general, do not come out looking like beauty contest winners. If you think about it, they have just gone through the birth canal, and their heads sometimes look a bit pointy. Not to mention the pinkish red color of their skin, and their eyes are closed with their noses all bunched up. That is how my dad saw my sister and me. Hearing that story said to me by Auntie Barb made me laugh. I think if he could have entered us into a beauty contest he would have. After taking a few minutes to pause while my sister and I got all cleaned up, he thought we were the most beautiful babies on the planet.

Dad already had the name Candace picked out, and they would nickname the child Candy. They pondered a name that sounded good with Candace; my mother came up with the name Constance, and the nickname would be Connie. Now, coming up with the middle names wasn't as difficult, as they decided to name both of us after my Dad's fraternal twin sisters, Sandra Sue, and Linda Lou. Since they already had the name Candace picked out; they decided to name the first-born Candace Lou and the second born Constance Sue.

I don't recall at what age my parents told me I was the first born and older twin, as it didn't matter. I think what was most shocking was that my mom didn't know she was having twins until she delivered, and then having to wait twenty-one minutes to push the second baby out is what resonates most of all. It's quite astonishing to me that my mom didn't have an epidural or any pain medication.

I remember growing up people would always ask my sister and me who was born first, and I wouldn't hesitate to spew out proudly, "I was, and I'm the oldest." It is so irrelevant and just silly to think I might have thought in my head that I had some advantage on my sister. We were, and always will be, different and unique in our ways, no matter the order. I now know there is no pecking order of an older or younger sibling. I think when we did learn about the order it was just innocent curiosity. Now, as for Mom, she would often remind us of the endurance she embraced waiting for Connie Sue to come out.

Bringing Twins Home While Faced with Unspeakable Tragedy

As my parents departed the hospital with my sister and me, I can only imagine the bit of panic they experienced, as they were only prepared to bring one home. They were not equipped, they only had one of everything, and now they were faced with having to buy two of everything. With twins also came double-duty for feeding, balancing time to bond, and building a one-on-one relationship with each child—not to mention caring for a toddler.

My parents had to make do with what they already had in place until they could buy two of what was needed to raise twins. They put us in the crib together until they could get a second one. I don't think they realized the demands of caring for two babies, but then again who would? They were delighted but also wondering how they were going to juggle the needs of their toddler and twins. Both were overwhelmed! It was apparent to them that accepting help from others when it was offered was key to getting my sister and me on a schedule.

When my parents brought my sister and me home, they felt a little guilty about not spending as much time with Danny as they did before. To make him feel just as important, they got him involved by assigning him simple tasks such as fetching diapers. Mom used to sing to my sister and me; Danny was included in on the hymns. One of my mom's favorite tunes she would sing to us was "Zip-a-dee-doo-dah," and Danny used to sing along. I can still envision her belting out the song off-pitch. Mom was no singer, but her heart was always in the right place.

She shared with my sister and me a funny story that to this day makes me pause and laugh. When you're a mother of twins and a three and a half-year-old, I am sure feeding your babies can be a challenge. By the time you finish feeding the babies, burp, and change them, before you know it the cycle begins all over again. It seemed back then mothers were not encouraged to breastfeed. She bottle-fed us as well as Danny, and he was an active, healthy little boy. This was a better option for my mom, as she could rely on help with the feeding from my dad; and Mom could get some relief during the middle of the night sessions.

When we finally could hold our bottles, our mother would hand us a bottle at bedtime in our crib. Mom soon realized that this didn't necessarily give her any reprieve before bed, as Connie used to steal my bottle and guzzle down whatever formula I might have left. Getting a second crib was much needed. Problem solved, at least you would think, right! We were growing, and our cribs were not that far from one another. Seemingly we were at a stage when we could pull ourselves up in the crib; Connie was darn resourceful, and I guess you could say a hungry baby. She used to stand up in the crib, scoot her way closer to me, and snatch my bottle away. Oh, the life of being a twin!

Writing this part is hard, to say the least. As a parent myself, I can't even possibly imagine the pain. Sadly, Danny was taken away from all of us when my sister and I were just a little over six weeks old. It was so sudden and unexpected, and deeply traumatizing on my parents, as well as their family and friends.

Danny drowned on July 17, 1962. He had wandered from our home down an open path that was established from the neighborhood worker who was using our water to assist in the building of a new home. That year there was lots of rain, and the grass was quite long. The workers made a footpath when they tromped through the thick brush. For a young boy, this trail was an attraction, and his curiosity is what set him out to see where it would lead him.

In the backyard of this house under construction, there was a seven-foot deep excavation ditch for a septic tank. Due to the massive rainfall, the hole filled up with water. To this day, so many unanswered questions remain somewhat of a mystery. My mom questioned her ability to be a good mother because she felt Danny's death was her fault. She would often say to me, "I wish I knew what was going through my sweet little boy's mind that day."

In that era, most houses were not built with an open floor plan. The kitchen and family room area were two different places. Mother was with Danny in the family room, and the phone rang. Within those few minutes when she was talking on the phone, Danny slipped out the back door. Mom also had just put my sister and me down for a nap. Upon hanging up minutes later, she found herself in a state of panic, as her little boy, my brother, was nowhere to be found in the house.

She called our neighbors hoping he went there, and in the meantime, she contacted my dad at work. Joni, screaming in fear, "Ron, I can't find Danny. He was just here, and now he's gone. I just put Candy and Connie down for a nap, and I was watching television with Danny in the family room. The phone rang; I answered it. He was only out of my sight for a few short minutes. Oh my God, where could he have gone?"

"I'm on my way home . . . in the meantime, contact the para-medics and keep looking for him!" Ron shouted in a state of panic.

Shortly after that, along with neighbors, everyone was search-ing for Danny. On the way home, my father's intuition was recalling the house still under construction, and that seven-foot-deep septic tank. Everything around him seemed to disappear or become very blurry. He couldn't drive fast enough to get to his son. His mind was swarming with so much anxiety as he was thinking the worst—afraid he had fallen in. He feared that the muddy water made the hole appear deceptively shallow looking and one of Danny's favorite pastimes, as with most young boys, was jumping in puddles and making a splash. When Ron arrived at the scene, he rushed to the hole fully clothed and plunged to the bottom where he found him. By this time, the Danville Fire Department Rescue Squad had arrived, and they worked to revive Danny for a half hour. They used three tanks of oxygen in their resuscitator. He was gone. How do you come to accept that you just lost your child?

Joni sobbed and repeatedly muttered, "Please don't take my baby!"

She was in a state of shock and disbelief, and so was my dad. She collapsed to the ground over his body, weeping, "They've taken my baby."

Neither one of them were in any shape to comprehend what had just happened.

Ron, crying, gently reached towards my mom, "Joni he is gone."

He held my mom for a few minutes, and they were in such disbelief as they kissed him on his forehead while they watched the paramedics carry their son away. It was a tragic accident. Neither one of my parents got over the pain and loss of losing their beautiful little boy. They had new twin daughters at home who had just arrived the month before. For them, they just experienced much joy having twins, and the loss of Danny must have felt like a nightmare, one from which they hoped they would wake up, and find Danny safely sleeping in his bed.

It was a very dark period for my parents. Both struggled with depression for some time. The simple activities like answering the phone, cooking dinner, getting the mail would cause them fear and anxiety, as they would continue to think that Danny was still among them. Coping with such a terrible misfortune was almost unbearable for them. They grieved in different ways. My mother became closed off because she didn't think she had the strength to take care of my sister and me. Unfortunately, my dad soothed his soul with alcohol. We all grieve differently, and each of us grieves at our pace. I suppose there is no timeline. At that time, my parents lost all hope for any spiritual comfort. They were mad at God and the world. How could God take their baby away, he was so little. Family and friends did what they could to help them get through this tragedy. Looking back, I know they were thankful for those caring and loving people in their lives.

My grandmother had never been on an airplane before, but she did so with Auntie Barb to be by my mom's side. She was thankful that my grandfather wasn't around to go through such pain and loss. Danny and Grandpa shared a special bond, and she was happy for what precious time they had with each other on their visits to Pittsburgh.

It was one thing for my mother having to say goodbye to her father but saying goodbye to her baby boy was unbearable. I can only imagine the sight of watching my dad carry him away, and the thought of a funeral would have been incredibly excruciating for both of them.

As the family arrived at Barrick and Son Funeral Home in Danville where the service took place, the atmosphere looked not only gloomy but also felt miserable. Everywhere my mother looked with her bleeding eyes there were no smiles.

"I hate this! Why would God take my baby?" Joni thought to herself as she took her seat in the front.

It seemed that anyone who knew came that day to offer his or her condolences. The line of people was endless, and although my mother was accepting everyone's sympathies, she felt she was having an out-of-body experience as if she wasn't there. I am sure that she was still in shock along with Dad. Grandma Doyle held my mom's hand throughout the entire funeral, saying to her, "It will be all right baby," but it was never all right, how does one ever get over the loss of a child? There is an old adage, "God doesn't give you what you can't handle," well, in this case, I am not so sure she or my father were equipped to deal with such a loss as the death of their son. I am relatively confident they were both mad at God.

There were rows and rows of chairs filled with family and friends. It was an open casket funeral. Danny looked so peaceful laid out in his coffin wearing one of Mom's favorite blue dapper short suits. Candles were lit that surrounded the casket, along with lots of beautiful flower arrangements. It was too unbearable for either one of my parents to get up in front of everyone to speak. For both, it was mostly a blur.

The moment had come where the service ended, and the casket was closed. Pallbearers carried Danny off to the hearse where he was taken to his final resting place. As the coffin lowered into the ground, many tears were shed. He was buried in Catlin at Oakridge Cemetery.

A wake was held at my grandparents' house in Danville. People came in and out, once again offering their condolences. My mom, in all honesty, wanted to skip this part, as all she wanted to do was curl up in a corner never to be seen again. Her life had been shattered by the loss of her son. It was exhausting for both of my parents having to face everyone; however, I know they were very thankful for every person that showed their support that day.

Connie and I were just infants, and she had little to no desire to care for us. Family and friends stepped in and helped them through this difficult time. I remember my mother always being overwhelmingly scared anytime she was around water, especially for Connie and me, as she thought that this random act of drowning could happen again. Thinking back, I am sure both my parents would have benefited from some professional counseling to help them cope with their loss. Getting past his death was extremely challenging for both of them, and it seemed that when they buried him, they also buried their thoughts because my dad could not talk about Danny.

Mom carried so much guilt of the loss of her son as she blamed herself since Danny was under her care at the time of his death. My dad never accused my mother, as we all know it was a tragic accident, but he carried a much heavier heart as he could not and would not speak of that terrible day. The subject matter was simply too painful for him. I remember when my sister and I were old enough to understand Danny was our older brother, and what happened, my dad wouldn't and couldn't talk to us about the events. My mom was the one who explained to us that we had a wonderful brother named Daniel Doyle Webb, and he went to live with the angels in heaven.

Over time, Danny's loss did soften, and their hearts began to heal. It seems that time helps heal our hearts. My mom's faith in God took many turns, but in the end, she found her way back to him in a manner stronger than she could ever imagine. I often think of Danny and wonder what kind of man he would have grown to be, and what it would have been like to have an older brother. I will always cherish the photos that we possess and the memories that my mother shared with my sister and me.

Joni found herself at a pivotal point in her life while working at the hospital as a surgical nurse. Although being a surgical nurse was her passion, the hours were becoming a hardship for her, as she forged on to raise my sister and me. Joni was on-call, and this warranted her to be on standby until she was called to work. Being that her hours were so unpredictable and she was

Daniel Doyle Webb—In Loving Memory (3½ years-old)

called-in at all hours, she knew she needed to find employment that would allow her to spend more time with her twins. She was determined to find a new position working as a nurse that would enable her to work regular hours, Monday through Friday.

William Hensold, M.D., (He was referred to by many as Dr. Bill.) needed a registered nurse to work beside him in his family practice office that he shared with, L.W. Tanner, M.D., and his wife Megan Tanner, M.D. It was a match made in heaven as she and Dr. Bill worked side-by-side up until he would retire.

Chapter 13

Family Connections

Many people who have either been adopted or in Mom's case, given away, grow up with a deep longing to reconnect with their biological family, but in Mom's case, she never had the desire to have any reunion with her biological family. I think what ultimately made the difference was Dorothy. At this point in Joni's life, there was no real threat of Iva ever trying to take her away, as she was a grown woman who was married with twins.

The year was 1971, and Iva became very ill. Over the years, Joni never formed a relationship with her. One day she received a phone call from her brother Jack. The information he relayed to my mom was a difficult choice for her to make.

"Hello, Joni, I just wanted to make you aware that Iva is in the hospital, and she is not expected to live. She has ovarian cancer. I don't know how you feel about coming to see her, but she is asking for you."

"Wow!" Joni paused in thought. "I'm not so sure how to respond, as I don't even know if I can get away."

"I'm certainly not calling you to put you on a guilt trip, and I would completely understand if you didn't come. I had to call and let you know either way."

"Well, I'm glad you did. Let me talk it over with Ron, and I will get back to you later today."

"Yes, of course, the nurses and doctors are ensuring that she is comfortable for now, but I have this feeling she is holding on so she can say goodbye to you. I will call you back shortly."

Suddenly Joni felt an aura of gray around herself; she was engulfed in sadness. It was completely different than when her daddy passed. A single tear rolled down her cheek. She was afraid if she didn't go she would regret it for the rest of her life. She felt that going to be by Iva's side very well might hurt her mother; the complete opposite was true, as Dorothy was my mom's strength, and she encouraged her to go. My dad also supported her decision.

Although this was a tough choice for her to make, I think she needed closure. She closed her eyes, trying to get the thought of Iva's impending demise out of her mind. For a moment, she felt guilty for not feeling a sense of deep remorse. Like it or not for so many years she tried to forget this woman, as her biggest fear growing up was that she would take her away from the Doyles.

In the end, she decided to go and see her. As one can imagine, it was another uncomfortable moment, especially knowing she would be seeing her helpless in a hospital bed, and it struck her that this would be the last time. So many questions had flooded her head before she arrived. What would she say? How long would she stay? Would all her brothers and sister be by her side? Who was her birth father? Unlike when her daddy was ill, she remained somewhat calm.

The lights were dimmed, and the door was propped open as Joni walked into Iva's room. An electronic machine sitting on a cart with all sorts of wires attached was monitoring her heartbeat. The bedside table had fresh, beautiful flowers that filled the air with a soft floral scent. Jack was there along with her siblings. She felt a genuinely warm greeting from Jack but not so much from the others. Iva was resting peacefully.

"Joni, I'm so glad you decided to come," Jack said.

"I appreciate you contacting me. Do you know how much time Iva has?"

"Well, the doctors are just trying to make her comfortable, and she didn't want to be so doped up that she wouldn't remember seeing you," Jack said.

Joni grabbed Iva's hand to let her know she was there. What surprised my mother was a charm bracelet that she was wearing. It was more apparent than ever that she indeed did somehow keep up with Mom over the years. Each charm was personalized with male and female heads, and they were engraved with all her grandchildren's names including Danny, myself, and Connie.

"Iva, it's Joni, I made it, I'm here," she whispered in her ear.

"I'm so glad you came." Iva squeezed her hand and turned her head towards Joni.

My mom was lost for words and not sure what to say. She hadn't thought about what she would say to her; mom didn't hold any bitterness towards Iva that she gave her away; but for the first time, Mom saw remorse in Iva's eyes.

"Joni, for mercy's sake you are not to blame. I am at fault, I didn't know what to do, but not a day has gone by that I didn't think about you. There are no words to express how much I love you. I hope you can forgive me!" Iva said, tears emerging from her eyes.

There was a lump in Joni's throat, "It's all right, and I forgive you. I suppose I am thankful for you putting me in the arms of the Doyles as they have been so good to me." Joni felt compassion for Iva, and her past actions should not add to her suffering. She had no ill feelings toward Iva. Iva must have spent years in agony over abandoning my mother when Joni was just an infant. Mom's hope that day was that she gave Iva some peace in realizing that Mom did have sympathy for her. My mom thought hard about seeing her and realized it was the right thing to do; after all, she gave her life.

Iva A. Goulding Johnson died of ovarian cancer on May 31, 1971. My mother was not by her side at the time of her death, nor did she feel compelled to attend the funeral, as she did not have a relationship with Iva. I suppose you could say it was complicated, not just for my mom, but for everyone else involved; however, what she did gain from this defining moment in her life was a brother.

A year or so had passed after the death of Iva, and annually my family would drive to Pittsburgh to spend time with Grandma Doyle and Auntie Barb. On this particular visit, Mom decided to meet up with her brother Jack, so we made the journey to Chambersburg, Pennsylvania, where he lived.

At this point in my life, she had explained the story of how Grandma Doyle was not our mom's birth mother. Although, thinking back to that day, we were too young to care. As for my mom, I remember her being extremely nervous in meeting with Jack once again, as she had ambivalent feelings towards him and her siblings.

Both Connie and I were used to long drives in our Ford station wagon. Grandma packed a picnic basket for all of us. It nestled nicely in the back of the car. There were no seat belts for anybody back then. The back of our car seats folded down, and we would make a bed to endure the time-consuming ride. It was about a three-hour drive to Chambersburg from Pittsburgh.

We gazed out the window and watched the cars go by one by one. Sometimes to pass the time we would play "Slug Bug"— whoever saw a Volkswagen Beetle drive by first would punch the other one in the arm shouting out "Slug Bug!" We would then keep a running score, and as I recall it was always a tight match. It was the funniest and cheapest pastime we could play in the back of a station wagon on extended drives.

When we finally arrived, we walked up to the door and rang the bell like strangers. For Connie and me this was another fun adventure, although for Mom she did her best to remain calm. I can faintly remember Jack greeting us at the door with so much enthusiasm.

"Come in, come in. How was your drive over?"

"Uneventful, except for the girls asking us over and over, 'are we there yet'?"

Meeting him for the first time, I can recall his features being very similar to my mother's. They both had olive tone complexion, black hair, and dark eyes. We went inside, and all the introductions began. Jack gave us all a big warm hug. I could feel the strength in his arms as he wrapped them around me.

"It's a pleasure to meet you both. Joni has told me great things about you girls. So how old are you?"

"We are ten years old." We said in unison.

"Meet my wife and kids."

"So, you're my mom's brother?" I spouted out.

"That's right, and that makes me your uncle."

It was a bit more complicated when he introduced all his kids to us. Jack had a son and daughter with his first wife and a son with his second wife. We also met a girl that Jack's wife had from her first marriage. We had never met anyone that had been married and divorced before. Looking back, we were all immediately thrust into the notion that these people were related to us. I think it was awkward for everyone. There was some sense of how can we possibly be bothered with this all these years later, as it seemed that everyone got on with their lives. I think for my mom and for her brother they found it to be an immense delight in their lives. For my sister and me, meeting our cousins just seemed fun and cool.

I imagine that meeting had a purpose. I don't remember much regarding that event, but I do recall meeting my mother's other siblings as they all lived in the general area. We, unfortunately, did not bond with them as we did with Jack. He became our "Uncle Jack" and a brother to Joni. My mom was so blessed to have met all her siblings but most of all being able to connect with her brother Jack.

His son Ben from his first marriage was living with them at the time. Ben was older than Connie and me by seven years. To us, we thought he was a "pretty cool dude." Sadly, we were not aware of the adversity that he faced growing up as a product of divorce. In my young eyes, I didn't quite understand what divorce was truly all about.

This encounter proved to be a success, as my mother and Jack had seemed to join as a family. My mom would finally have a sibling that she would grow close to. What also came from this visit were our family annual vacation trips to Treasure Island, Florida. Both Connie and I have very warm-hearted reminiscences of our trips to the Sunshine State.

Vacation was something that my parents held very dear to them. My sister and I have vivid recollections of Uncle Jack being so jovial and cheerful around us. He loved us, and that was something we always felt from him. We could sense the pride he shared in getting to know Mom and our family. Our family vacations together truly confirmed that. Dad would race Uncle Jack to get to our sanctuary spot where we met every year, same time, and same place—Trails End Resort. Once again, for Connie and me, we would have to gear up for yet another long drive playing "Slug Bug." The car would be loaded down with what seemed like our entire wardrobe and a cooler full of food. As soon as the wheels rolled, of course, the anticipation instantly morphed into "Are we there yet?"

I used to think of our road trips as a moment to share some family fun time and lore. With all that time spent in a car, we often heard lots of storytelling from Mom and Dad, not to mention our dad trying to impose such ridiculous orders as no bathroom breaks. Of course, driving with all girls in the car, he typically didn't win out on that rule. I suppose that is why he would inherently lose the competition in making it to the finish line before my Uncle Jack.

As children, my sister and I were impatient travelers, and I'm sure my folks did everything they could to make the long journey the best they could for the whole family. There were times when they let us take a friend on the trip. Being twins, we were competitive and somewhat argumentative. By allowing a friend to join in on our adventure, they would put her in the middle to separate my sister and me. Looking back, I can appreciate their thought in allowing us to bring along a pal, as we were always full of excitement having a best friend going on this wild vacation with us; it was a great treat. I'm sure we all still whined, "Are we there yet?" often enough to drive my parents nuts, but those aren't the only memories that linger.

On one occasion, I can recall our friend, Lisa Barkman, going with us to Treasure Island. She spent a lot of time with my family from a very young age. We met in fifth grade and remain, friends today. We all couldn't wait to make our first stop, as that meant slipping into our bathing suits and racing to the pool to show off our dives. We couldn't get there fast enough. We were running so fast that as my sister went towards the glass door continuing to sprint and BAM, her face hit the door so hard that she fell backward and her eyes got moist.

I'm sure my sister was so embarrassed. Lisa and I fell to the floor, and we were laughing so hard. Luckily, she didn't really get hurt. To loosen the tension, we helped her up and reassured her that nobody else was around to see her hit the door bouncing back like a punching bag. I do have to defend my sister as it could have happened to any of us, as the glass was crystal clear. We did wonder if they polished the door for hours every day?

The next morning, we were even more excited, as our next stop was breakfast. Now being a mother, and not to imply I am a super mom wearing a cape, but it can be challenging when compromising over choices our children make when they are old enough to read a menu, not to mention the pictures that are depicted on the list of options, making the food appear mouthwatering. What do we see as kids that we can't resist? It was a most luscious image of a stack of pancakes filled with chocolate chips, heavily sprinkled with powdered sugar, crowned with whipped cream and Hershey's syrup dripping off the sides; it was a must have!

"Mom . . . please, oh please, can we have the chocolate chip pancakes?"

We screamed relentlessly.

Like most mothers, my first inclination is NO, and not just no, but HELL NO! One would like to think that you are once again a super mom and will not let them wear you down. The soft hearted man that my dad was, well let's just say, he had some influence on helping us campaign for those flapjacks.

"Joni, what can it hurt, we are on vacation; let the girls have the chocolate chip pancakes."

"Ron, you think it's a good idea to fill their bellies full of sugar on the long drive we have ahead of us? Aside from that, we have plenty of treats in the car." She reminded him.

"Pretty please, we have never had chocolate chip pancakes before."

"I said no," my mother replied, while she buried her head in the menu hoping that we would stop whining.

Our little faces were unhappy, and our upper lips curled up in sadness. Then our next strategy was to drop a tear, and in between wiping our cries, we all delivered a gasp of air, purely for effect.

"Fine, you can have the chocolate pancakes, but on one condition. You have to eat every last bite, you hear me!"

Of course, our sad faces turned to smiles, and we couldn't wait to sink our teeth into those pancakes. Our plates arrived, and we dug in, "Mm! Mm! Good!" was our first thought. What we did not anticipate was just how sickeningly sweet it was and how, as usual, our eyes were bigger than our stomachs. We knew that by not finishing our plates, we would be in for a tongue-lashing, so we had to buck up and eat it all. We learned a good lesson that day, as we thought we were going be sick to our stomachs! We ate every bite, unfortunately, for my parents; they had to endure our moaning.

To drown us out, Dad would play his favorite jam on the radio, singing loudly to the one and only Johnny Cash whom he held in such high regard. The CB radio was a craze when we used to make those long drives, and both our parents would talk to truck drivers as well as Uncle Jack. Mom's handle was "Bubbles." She used to be the one who would converse, as apparently, the truck drivers seemed to be enthralled more so when they heard a woman's voice over the airwaves.

"Breaker, breaker 1-9." Bubbles said.

"Come on little lady, how can I help you?" A truck driver replied.

"Just checking if there are any Smokeys on the highway, 10-4," in a very covert way, my mom would tell him in CB lingo where our location on the highway was.

"Affirmative there little lady, what's your location?"

The truck driver would tell her there was a Smokey on our back door, or he would say, "Put your peddle to the metal, all clear!" We always had so much fun!

At last, we would finally make it to the finish line, and when Dad would pull into the resort's parking lot and see Uncle Jack's car, he would chuckle and spew out a few cuss words making it known to all of us that we lost the race. Our days started with my parents getting the best umbrella table nearest to the pool. They would sip on their "cup of Joe" gearing up for a long day of beer drinking.

Shuffleboard was by far their favorite pastime. It seemed that this game was popular in the sunny communities of Florida. There were several courts lined up side by side, and you sometimes had to wait in line to use them. Each team takes their stand on either side of a 39-foot long concrete court. They take turns pushing four discs aiming for a triangular zone to earn points and the first to score 75 wins. If you would ask my dad who won, he was always the champion. No matter what the outcome my dad and Uncle Jack bonded over this memorable game.

By the end of a most joyous and fun day of hanging out by the pool and the beautiful Gulf of Mexico, Lisa, my sister, and I would get gussied up in our infamous bib overalls accompanied with a tube top. Back in the 1970s and early 1980s, this was a distinctive look. It was a fashion statement, and we were proud to wear our outfits for everyone to see. Dad, on the other hand, hated this style and he and Uncle Jack conjured up a plan to try to break us of wearing this hip design.

Looking back, I can laugh and reminisce of this now, because at the time I think we all hated it. The experience always ended in us screaming, and my father and Uncle Jack laughing until their stomachs hurt. We were a tangle of frustration and fury, as they would grab us and push us into the pool. For teenage girls, it always takes quite a bit of time to get fixed up, hair was done up and such, so when we came out of that pool, we were in a rage as that meant we had to shower and fix our hair all over again. We learned our lesson the hard way, as to ensure that we didn't wear our bibs and tube top anywhere near the pool ever again.

I can visualize my family and the people we encountered on our long awaited fabulous Florida vacations. Dad was a tall skinny man who was proud to prance around in his red-hot swim trunks and Uncle Jack bearing his robust belly for everyone to see. Mom would wear her hand-crocheted string bikinis that she made. When we were there, we owned the hotel; it was ours for those two glorious weeks. Because our family was so small, it was wonderful getting to know our true biological relatives.

Connecting with a Special Cousin and Nephew

Although Ben was not a part of the wonderful family vacations we would share with his father, he was someone who very much became the fabric of our lineage. We were all so blessed that he came into our lives, as he made our family so much richer than what it already was. The year was 1975, and Ben was eighteen years old still living with Uncle Jack and his wife, Pat, in Chambersburg, Pennsylvania. He worked for a vending company at the time, and back then, it wasn't as challenging to find a job. The hours, on the other hand, were less than desirable for a young man of eighteen, as Ben had to get up at 4:00 am and report to

Left to right: Lisa Knight, Connie Mitchell, Candy Henderson

work by 5:00 am. He had a route where he serviced the drink, candy, and food machines, located mostly in the dorms of a college in Shepherdstown, West Virginia. A fair amount of his workday was spent driving, as most of his territory was remote.

Upon arrival on campus, he would drive the truck full of reloads for the machines, to the closest door possible. Three of the dorms were women's only and back then for a young male adult that was considered a great gig. Per the instruction of the Dean, who was a relatively laid-back guy, Ben would have to enter the dorms through the service door making as much noise as possible alerting the girls he was present to do his business, stocking the vending machines.

Left to right: Ron, Candy, Connie, & Joni

"Man, in the hall!" he pauses and waits a moment.

"Man, in the corridor!" Ben shouted.

It was 1976; it was a time when some young women were not overly concerned about being seen less than fully dressed while entering, and leaving showers, etc. As Ben recounted the story to me, he was perhaps somewhat naïve for wanting out of this job, and even the area. As Ben eventually learned the hard way, there are some harsher ways to earn a living out there should one find oneself desperate and hungry enough; but then again, who knew "era of peace and love" from the 1960s and 1970s was going to end and revert to more conservative convictions.

For Ben, this was a year or so of his life where he became close to my Uncle Jack, who was his father. Uncle Jack was not too fond of some of his friends. Ben had very long hair all through high school; he let himself fall from being a 4.0 GPA student to almost not graduating, mostly because he had no direction, little ambition, maybe the wrong friends, and not much in the way of confidence from his family. As a younger child, he lived with his mother who eventually remarried; on weekends he would stay with his father, his wife, her daughter, and soon enough their son. A year later his mother had another son. As a young girl, I could not quite understand the whole dynamics of the situation at the level I do now as an adult, but little did I know at the time, nor did my mother, that she would change his destiny.

I'm sure it also didn't help Ben's situation with his parents that he kept wild hours, and his transportation was a thunderous Harley Davidson. His parents would receive phone calls from more than several neighbors a week about his loud motorcycle in the middle of the night. Since he wasn't home much of the time, they had to deal with it and likely wonder who was sleeping under their roof. He had the bad boy image down to a 'T' because it was who he had become those last few years. I know Ben feels he surely could have been a better son. When he did finally hold down a steady job and did it well, I'm sure it must have put Uncle Jack at ease. I think all Ben was looking for was his father's respect, even though he still refused to get a haircut. In his mind, Uncle Jack hoped that just maybe his son wouldn't end up a bum after all.

During this year or so, Ben wrote letters to a friend of his, coincidently by the name of Ron. He was in the Navy, who at the time happened to be stationed in Long Beach, California. His letters seemed to be endless rants about how beautiful all the California girls were, and how he needed to come and check out the "scene." Ron was planning to use his entire 30 days of leave to get back to Pennsylvania where he would buy a van and catch

Ben and Uncle Jack enjoying a boat ride on Lake Wylie

up on some of the activities he and his gang had been up to that landed him in the military. They eventually were pounded by the local law, fessed up to their wrongdoing, and paid restitution for some hunting cabins in the mountains they had broken into for alcohol and whatnot. At the time, Ron was the only one who was eighteen, and since he was legally considered an adult, he was looking at a record if he didn't heed the suggestion of the judge, who explained how the military would be a good experience for a wayward young man.

They intended no harm, and when he came back, they all had learned that lesson, but they wanted to be young free guys again, and thus, they began to hatch a plan to venture out to sunny Southern California. On their way out, much to our surprise, Ben and his friend stopped by our home as they were passing by, heading west. The year was 1976, and Connie and I were 14 years old. I remember him being so cool and thinking to myself, "Wow, how lucky he is to be moving to California near the majestic deep blue Pacific Ocean."

Crazy to think years later that is just what I did. They were packed and ready to go. Ben's friend Ron drove the van with all their belongings, and Ben straddled on his Harley Davidson trailing behind. There was no timeline on their trip out west, but one thing for sure was that Ben wanted to make a stop and visit his Aunt Joni. They both aspired to camp; they wanted to ensure that they see Yellowstone and the Badlands.

I can't imagine riding a motorcycle from the East Coast to the West Coast, but Ben was determined. He recalls the bugs were so thick when he was passing through Indiana and Illinois that he rode approximately eight inches behind the van. Ben used the vehicle as a shield to help with his vision, as the bug guts were so thick he couldn't keep them cleaned off his face shield so he could see; Ben prayed Ron didn't have to make a quick stop—Ben knew what he was doing was pretty risky. Fortunately, it worked out, and they made it to our doorstep.

When Ben and Ron arrived, they tentatively tapped on the door, "tap . . . tap . . . tap." Aunt Joni answered the door and there stood Ben and Ron, a welcome sight. They looked tired; everyone was so happy to see one another. My dad, being the proud Marine he was, to say the least, immediately started swapping military stories with Ron. Ben and my mom chatted away looking for answers to many unanswered questions about the Goulding family. Sadly, Ben was still young, and he didn't take as much interest in the lineage as Mom did, not to mention the divorces where Ben was caught in the middle and instantly had stepsisters along with half-brothers.

It seemed that Ben's history was far too complicated for even him to keep it straight, let alone try to explain to his Aunt Joni. For Ben, it took very little time to know that his Aunt Joni was so precious, loving, and a strong woman. Her entry into a room demanded attention, and if anyone knew my mom, that's just who she was. The next day Connie and I spent a little time with our new cousin. He probably learned a bit more than he wanted to know, as we talked his ear off.

They stayed in Danville for a couple of days, as the chill of winter was in the air, and they were taking the northern route for the next few legs of their trip. Snow in the Rockies on a motorcycle is not a good combination. They said their goodbyes and rolled out; Ben was left thinking about my mom, and he realized he now had more family than he thought. I remember Mom being so genuinely concerned about what Ben was going to do with his life. She was sincerely worried, as was Ben, but he had a hard time thinking much ahead of tomorrow. That openly emotional caring was something he wasn't experienced in dealing with. At this point, he wondered if maybe she'd been fortunate, in a way, not being raised in the turmoil and endless drama that was in Chambersburg for his family when he was growing up.

He was living the California dream. Being from the Midwest, I was obsessed with the idea of life in California. I am sure Ben held on to the hope the West Coast would be where he would settle. It was certainly a giant leap of faith on his part, which led him out west. He was living the American Dream. He managed to get a job and settle in for several great years. The fastest lesson he learned living as a Californian is that it was expensive to live there. He struggled as most do to pay the rent. There is no question that California has the best weather in the world—particularly Southern California. He had a fantastic time and loved living in Manhattan Beach. Two short blocks from a world-class beach on a steep hillside, the view at sunset was the orange evening sun illuminating the entire dining room/living room and kitchen of the reflection of the great Pacific Ocean. While he lived there, he learned and grew, as his eyes, heart, and mind opened to another way of life.

In 1978, he decided to leave the West Coast and head back to Chambersburg. He found himself at a crossroads in his life that would ultimately send him to my mom. He had to make a difficult decision to leave and head back to his roots.

When he showed up on our doorstep, I don't think anyone in my family realized he would become such a special nephew to my mom and an actual cousin to my sister and me. He came to us a confused and angry young man with not much good to offer the world. At least that's what he thought at the time. Mom took him in, and she believed in him when no one else did. She shared a special kind of love and wisdom with him. When it was time for him to depart, he left us as a humble man who I know to this day feels my mother forever changed his destiny. She gave him the strength to move on to better things in his life, and a gift to all of us for him being a part of our family.

Chapter 14

Selling the House of Love

Years passed by, and Grandma Doyle was still successfully running her boarding house without her beloved Frank. There was a sudden hollow echo of knuckles rapping on her front door. Grandma was washing the dishes when she heard the banging. She slowly moved her aging body up the stairs and opened the front door.

"Hello, my name is Roy, I am looking for a room to rent, and I saw your sign in the window. Is it still available?"

"Why yes, it is, come on in, and we can discuss it."

At first glance, Roy appeared to be a polite and friendly young man. It was noticeable that he had a cleft palate and it affected his speech. It was apparent to Grandma he was somewhat self-conscious of his speaking, so much so he would use his hands to cover his mouth when talking to her. Being the easy-going and caring woman she was, she felt compassion for him. She then explained the rules, as she did with all her past and present tenants about what her expectations were living under her roof.

He began by telling her that he was an orphan, and he didn't have much money. When he was born, his mother didn't want him because of his cleft palate, and therefore, he had been a ward to the state. Sadly, he was brought up in a children's home. As Roy grew older living with a noticeable cleft palate, he realized that his birth family didn't want him because of how he looked, and no one ever reclaimed him. It would make sense why Grandma took to him.

"I don't have much of an income, but whatever I can't pay you in rent, I was hoping that you might need someone to help out around the house. You know, I could be your maintenance guy."

This touched Grandma Dorothy's heart, as it reminded her of her early adulthood when she took in my mother. Although it was under different circumstances, she realized the distress and anxiety that he must have felt growing up; therefore, her heart ached for this young man. I believe fate brought Roy to my grandma.

"Oh my gosh, I am so sorry, but around here you don't have to be ashamed of your disability, as we are all unique in our own ways. I'm sure we can work something out. What are your suggestions?"

"I can only afford to pay you half the rent each month, but I will work for you to pay off the remaining amount. I can do any general maintenance and repairs you might need around the house. I will go to the grocery store for you, whatever you need help with."

"Well, that sounds good to me. I could certainly use an extra hand around here. Shall we give it a trial run? Let's say a 30-day temporary period. If it works out for both of us, I would be happy to have you as a permanent tenant."

"Thank you so much, Mrs. Doyle! I promise I won't let you down. When can I move in?"

"Well, as soon as you are able; today if you can."

She quickly took to Roy and he to her, she often referred to him as the boy she never had. Although Roy was never able to pay a full month's rent, he kept his promise and worked it off. Having him live with Dorothy was a huge help to her. After all, she was not getting any younger, and my mom would worry about her taking care of that big house since her daddy passed away. My grandmother was the nicest person, and having Roy staying with her, was a bit of relief to my mom.

When Joni first met Roy, it was evident he loved and respected my grandma. He had a kind heart and always did his best to please her by doing chores, such as caring for the lawn and garden, shoveling snow in the winter and many other house duties. He became her right-hand man. My mom could see for herself the difficulty in understanding Roy's speech due to his upper palate never closing properly. I'm sure he was made fun of growing up, and he was probably very embarrassed when meeting people for the first time.

Roy was very aware of his disability, but around Grandma and my mom, they accepted him. Roy was so appreciative, and to show it he was very dutiful with any household chores around the house that needed attention. Despite all his hardships and mocking growing up, it was unbelievable just how big-hearted he was; all he ever wanted out of life was to fit in. Roy remained with my grandmother until one day she knew the house was getting to be too much for her to manage. Dorothy was getting old in age, and her health was beginning to deteriorate. Grandma was certainly a fighter, and for the better part of her life, she was extremely healthy. She didn't like going to get regular checkups and didn't go to the doctor's unless it was absolutely necessary. Having Roy living in the house all those years was comforting not only to Grandma but to my mom. He would often call my mom to keep her abreast of how she was doing.

It wasn't easy for Grandma to come to the realization it was time to sell the big house on Neville Street; when she finally made up her mind to do so, we knew she would be picky about finding the right buyers. This house was a "house of love"; she viewed it as a sanctuary of peace, it was cozy and safe. There was a definite feeling of relief when you entered the home after being away; it was home to where she cared for so many children. The warmth of Frank, her beloved husband, and most importantly her daughter Joni filled the house. This home had played many roles for Grandma Dorothy over the years, but its comforts were defined by simple, blissful moments like these. She lived in the Neville Street house for thirty-eight years.

With much thought and reservations, she concluded it was time to sell. She had many different buyers come through the house, all with good intentions, but she refused to sell to just anyone. It had to be the perfect buyer. She wanted to make sure whoever bought the house would maintain and restore it for people in need of a place to live. In less than six months, she finally found the perfect buyer and it was sold.

It just so happened that there was a group of community leaders and doctors who would purchase my grandmother's house. The home, at 514 North Neville Street is now the Family House Neville; one of three all located in the Pittsburgh area. Dorothy's vision continues to live on there. It warms my heart that today that very same house serves as a temporary home for families whose loved ones are undergoing treatment nearby in Pittsburgh. It is fitting to see so many in need being sheltered, lovingly in the home where my mother grew up and my grandmother cherished. This seventeen-room boarding house served as a home to many people from most every circumstance and these people were very much a foundation of who my mother grew to be.

I am sure that Roy was so grateful for Grandma taking a chance on him all those years ago, and I am thankful that they

Joni visiting the Family House, 2011

had each other. Once the house was sold in 1989, Grandma was instrumental in assisting Roy in getting a great job as a caretaker for a well-established apartment building located on Craig Street. Funny how Craig Street comes full circle, as the first house where the Doyles began their venture taking in babies was located on Craig Street. Roy was so thankful to Dorothy; he was finally able to save his money, and he would invest his money wisely, as Grandma did. Along with the job, he also was provided with health insurance. He always wanted to get his cleft palate fixed, but he couldn't afford it. Having insurance finally allowed him to improve his disability to some degree.

Roy was well respected at the apartment complex he maintained. Even after he accepted the job, he always checked in on my grandma each week. He helped with anything she needed. Mom was so grateful for so many people who came into her life and my grandmother's life, and Roy was one of those extraordinary people.

Grandma rented a studio apartment right behind the house on Neville Street. It was located on Bayard Street; she could look out her window and see the progress happening at the Family House. Dorothy felt extremely fortunate her new place was close by; I think this helped her move on and appreciate her cherished house would be valued by people who needed a place to stay. During the summer months, she slowly strolled over with her cane in hand to sit on her much-loved nostalgic front porch. The surroundings looked a little different. The beautiful rose bushes that lined her veranda were gone. Tranquility would describe her memories of her time spent on that porch. The landscape of the house might have changed a bit, as would the facades of buildings and the faces of the people that would pass through.

Change is necessary, but what will never change is the love that the house still has to offer. I have no doubt that for a long time to come, the people who are fortunate enough to experience staying in the house will leave with some sense of gratitude. Whether it is sitting on the front porch for a little fresh air, a little conversation, to settle in a chair, it will always be a place for pause and a place to heal. My grandma's hard work and giving back finally paid off in the end.

Grandma was an adamant and independent woman who never really accepted much advice from others on what she should or should not do. She was not one to make doctor visits. Dorothy's health began to deteriorate progressively. She developed a severe illness, but being the stubborn woman she was, refused to see a doctor. Mom knew she had to make a trip to escort her to a health care provider and fast. She was complaining of black stools and discomfort in her abdomen. When Mom arrived, she saw she had lost quite a bit of weight; she knew Grandma was sick and in trouble. Joni was notorious for self-diagnosing everyone; I think it came from being a nurse. However, this was her mom, and it was critical she get her to a medical provider at once to get her a proper diagnosis. This time she knew speculation was a bad idea.

After months of Grandma not feeling well, she went to see a doctor at Shadyside hospital, where she was diagnosed with colon cancer. The doctor had no other options other than to take out much of her colon. Thus, she would have to live her remaining years with a colostomy bag. For most people adjusting to a colostomy bag is a daunting experience, but Grandma felt blessed they were successful in removing her cancer; so, if this meant that she would have to live with a colostomy bag, it was something she would have to get used to. Mom ended up staying with her for a little over two months to assist her with managing her colostomy bag. Grandma developed a way to accept her colostomy bag; she named it "Oscar." Whenever she was out, she'd say, "Well ladies, I have to run and take care of Oscar."

Many of her friends never even knew she had a colostomy bag. She was not one for sympathy. No one asked who Oscar was, so they all assumed she had a male friend to take care of. Her recovery process was relatively smooth. She was lucky, as she did not have to undergo any chemotherapy or radiation treatments, not to mention she was now pain-free. My mom pleaded with Grandma to come and live with her, but she kept telling her she was not ready yet. It was hard for my mom to leave Grandma when she did, but Mom had to get back to work and her life in Danville.

On her next trip back to see Grandma, she encountered the custodian of the apartment complex where she lived. As I look back and recall the story, it is comical as she referred to her colostomy bag as Oscar; he thought Dorothy had a boyfriend that she helped. I can only imagine her astonishment when he told Mom about Grandma's gentleman friend, as it turned out Grandma was referring to her old friend Oscar the colostomy bag. This was a much needed all around good laugh they both shared that day in the lobby. He never knew about her colostomy bag until my mom clarified who Oscar was.

When Mom would visit Grandma Doyle, she would spend much of her time cleaning her apartment from top to bottom to ensure she wouldn't worry about anything. For my mom, it kept her busy and her mind off Grandma's illness. Mom knew she was living on borrowed time, and she knew one day that her mother could take an unexpected turn for the worse. This is something I know we all try to prepare ourselves for when we are caring for our aging parents, but we don't realize the impact it will have on us until faced with the reality.

The year was 1991, and my mom received a phone call from Grandma, telling her that she was not well. Mom knew in her heart things were not right, and this might be her final trip back to Pittsburgh to see her mother. Grandma was admitted to the hospital, and it was determined that the cancer was back. Mom pleaded with her mother to take her back to Danville. She was finally ready to make the trip with her. It's hard to believe my mom was so determined to get her home that she would arrange for a private plane to fly her there. Mom safely transported her to Lakeview Hospital in Danville. Mom was optimistic Grandma would get well enough to go home with her. I think Grandma knew this would be her final journey, and she agreed to go back with Mom as she had begged her for so many years to come and live with her. Grandma must have known it was her time and she must have known she couldn't stop this fight and Mom couldn't prevent her death; for that matter nobody could. It wasn't until later my mom realized her mother was going to die. Dorothy was ready, and even when she knew her death was imminent, she would joke with my mom saying, "One thing I know for sure Baby, Oscar will not get into heaven but I will. I am ready to see my loving Frank and most of all, your sweet Danny boy."

She only lasted four days in the hospital, and she would pack up her bags and make her final journey to her next rooming house, heaven. Dorothy started out her passage as a renter in a boarding house, then a foster mother, and eventually owning and operating her rooming house for folks who didn't have a lot. Now, her home of thirty-eight years lives on, and anyone who is a family member of someone receiving medical treatment can seek out affordable housing in a homelike environment at the Family House Neville.

I am proud, as her granddaughter, that this woman dedicated much of her life to helping others. So much so that she raised my mom, Joni Doyle, to become the caring and nurturing mother to my sister and me. The Neville House, along with several other homes in the surrounding area are established to help those in need of temporary, affordable housing while their loved ones are undergoing treatment. Dorothy Doyle lives on in that house. I honestly believe she lingers, as an angel, ensuring the house on

Neville will forever bring calmness for families to enjoy a quality of life while their loved ones are in the hospital. Dorothy Doyle passed away on August 12, 1991; may her soul rest in peace forever.

Mom had to ensure Grandma returned to Pennsylvania to be buried next to her beloved Frank. This time she was transported in a hearse from Danville, Illinois to Pennsylvania. I never asked, nor did I question my mom on the cost associated with the transport. I often wondered why she went through all the trouble of bringing her back to Danville, only to die; however, in the end, that is what she wanted, and I respected her decision. At the time, I was living in the Chicago area, and I flew with my mom to Pennsylvania to support her in making Grandma's funeral arrangements. Grandma was a simple lady; she did not want the fuss of a funeral where people would come and view her body. Her wishes were to be buried in a beautiful baby blue negligée. I remember her once saying, "When I die, don't put a fancy dress on me; I am going to sleep, so you better put me in a nightie."

Looking back, it makes sense. I often wonder if going to sleep every night is like being dead. We are not self-aware while we are sleeping and we are not aware of our surroundings. I must ask myself the question, is sleeping a similar thing to being dead? My grandmother looked so peaceful as if she was in a deep, deep slumber. There was a sense of peace her face portrayed as she was tucked away in her casket. Her eyes were closed as if she were going to bed; I touched her hands as they laid across her belly folded in prayer. My mom and I gave her a final kiss on her forehead. It was so peaceful; it was just my mom and me all alone saying our last goodbyes.

Dorothy Mae Doyle was a woman never to be forgotten. That day the world lost a real treasure. She was to be buried alongside her darling Frank at St. John's Lutheran Church in

Connoquenessing, Pennsylvania. It has been a tradition every year since the death of my grandpa that on Memorial Day their graves be decorated with beautiful flowers to grow and flourish during the spring and summer months. It seemed the right thing to do since they had such adoration for flowers. My sister and I carry on that same tradition out of respect for our mother and our grandparents.

Frank and Dorothy's final resting place

Chapter 15

Oh, The Places She Would Go

The years somehow got away from all of us as they do; my mom moved on. At this point in her life, she and my dad were divorced. I don't think my dad ever actually recovered from the loss of my brother and for him to cope, he drank. Although, as hard as it was for my mom to realize that she couldn't go on enabling him, finally, she had to let him go. It was at this time when I understood what divorce was all about. For my sister and me, it was hard for us to grapple with the fact that our parents were divorcing. Although we didn't want to imagine them separated, we knew it was imminent. When my parents decided to split, my sister and I were young adults. We were better equipped to grasp the situation, but that didn't mean it hurt us any less. What we did know is that neither one of them was happy.

My dad did re-marry sometime after my parents divorced, but one thing I am certain of is that my dad never stopped loving my mother up until the day he passed away from lung cancer. How I know this is he used to profess his love for my mother saying, "You know I still love your mother, and I always will."

As much as I wished my parents had been able to live their remaining years out together, I realize now that it had to be the way it was. I am thankful my dad found that someone he was able to spend his remaining years with. As for my mom, she would fall in love with a man she cherished from a far.

It seemed so sad to me; although my father moved on with someone else, deep down I think he regretted their divorce. I truly believe the loss of his son set him on a path of sadness that he just couldn't quite ever get over, which led to his excessive drinking. He died on March 27, 2004, with my sister and me along with his second wife by his side. My father's wishes were to be buried beside his precious Danny boy located in Catlin at Oak-wood Cemetery.

My mom continued to work for Dr. Hensold at his family practice as his nurse. He was instrumental in getting her through those rough couple of years after their divorce. Working as a caregiver was therapeutic for Mother. She was a nurse through and through—a "nurse with unmatchable service." Her individual care and regard for people and families set the gold standard in Danville. She was like a rock star, as it seemed that wherever we went in that town, she would typically be mobbed with attention from her former patients.

One of her precious pastimes was playing golf. She had such a love for the game. She tried to teach me how to play, but I never became the avid golfer that she was. She was well-known on the golf course. You could see her from a mile away, with her tall stature sporting her beautiful silver locks. She embraced her gray hair. I guess you could say she had to, as her tresses started turning silver in her late teens. Growing up, all I remember is her beautiful bright, shining hair that reflected the light. Welcoming gray hair isn't for every woman, but the ranks of those who choose freedom from artificial color and the tyranny of monthly touch-ups are admirable. Personally, I haven't resolved myself in joining the ranks of those women. I am sure that day will arrive, but for now, I choose color! My mom, however, pulled it off, always looking great with her silver white hair wearing a sophisticated style.

Mom would continue to live life to the fullest. Nothing would stop this force of nature. However, after 29 years of service working as Dr. Hensold's nurse, she retired in 1992 at the young age of 56. That, however, didn't mean that she was ready to hang up her nurse's cap. She lived for her children and her grandchildren. The family was everything to my mom. She would finally move from the tiny town of Danville to be near my family and me in the northern suburbs of Chicago. She took on the adventure of building a home on a lake in Lindenhurst, Illinois. She also wasted no time in getting herself a job at a nearby skilled nursing facility. Her motto was if she could work as a nurse, she saw no reason in stopping what she loved so dearly.

My family and I lived nearby in a house that we also had built in Grayslake, Illinois, until one day my husband was faced with being transferred back to California. The year was 1997, and I had just welcomed my second child, a girl named Carly Joan. It was hard to believe that we were being relocated again. It seemed each time I got pregnant we moved, as when I delivered my son, Devin Doyle, in 1990, we were reassigned from California to the Chicago area.

Oh gosh, how would I break this news to my mom? She was now 61 years old, and she had only lived in her brand-new house for a few years. She was just getting her house decorated to perfection. It was important to her to make her home cozy. Each dwelling she ever owned, she decked it out with color. She kept up with the trends. When wallpaper was in, every room was adorned with colorful paper. I think if she were to have taken up another career, it would have been an interior designer. Off we went to sunny Southern California in search of a home for my family as well as my mom; she decided to pick up and move across the country with us. She was not afraid of adventure, that's for sure.

I remember when we arrived in sunny Southern California; it wasn't so sunny. It was an El Nino year with lots of rain. We started out looking at houses in the Orange County area until we got an unexpected phone call from my husband. We had to shift gears and spend the remaining time looking in an entirely different county, as he was being transferred to a different part of the company located in Colton.

"Colton . . . where the hell is Colton!" was my response.

I began to cry, as I didn't want to live any other place except Orange County. How could this be happening? I didn't want to live in the Inland Empire. Heck! I didn't even know where the Inland Empire was; all I knew was the coastal area.

To calm me down he said, "Several of my new co-workers told me there is a quaint town on the way to Palm Springs, called Redlands."

Again, I had never heard of Redlands; I just knew that I had an uneasy feeling about moving to Redlands, and I didn't want to go; now we had to find a realtor who was familiar with the area. It was surprising how flexible and open she was to look wherever we needed. Much to our surprise, we could get a much larger home for our money in Redlands as opposed to Orange County, so we began our pursuit.

We were lucky to find a great team who helped us with our move. It made me much more at ease about the move when I discovered the locals described it as "The Jewel of the Inland Empire." My mother and my family were both able to find homes. Mom's house was located on La Flora and mine on Magnolia.

We only lived a few miles from one another. Mom dove in and redecorated yet another home, and within a matter of weeks, she landed a job as an RN working in a skilled nursing facility.

We had finally decorated our new homes just the way we wanted; then one day here comes Mom, she barged into our house yelling,

"Candy, you have to come and look at this house I just toured, it's beautiful!"

"Umm, okay but why would we move, we just got our homes the way we want them?"

"I know, but it doesn't hurt to look, now does it?"

Off we went; the further up the hill we traveled, the bigger the houses got. We pulled up in front of this dwelling, and it was huge. It had a big beautiful wraparound front porch, just like what Mom grew up with on Neville Street. Even before entering the house, I knew the porch is what caught her attention. It was a one-hundred-year-old, three story, seven bedroom, four bath, and 4,376 square foot Heritage Award winning Dutch Colonial built by architect Gordon Donald. The house had so much character with coffered ceilings, crown molding, with trim-finish work, and of course the wrap-around porch leading into the spacious formal entry. On the main floor, there was a formal living room with a wood-burning fireplace, a dining area with solid wood pocket doors along with a beautiful chandelier. One of the large bedrooms had another fireplace we used as a theater room. The kitchen was in the back of the house on the main floor; off the kitchen, was a large den area and a bathroom. The room featured large windows that overlooked the pool/spa in a spacious backyard with access to the garden on a finished deck. In California to have a large yard is premium; the home also had a basement, which is almost unheard of in California.

Redlands Home when we bought it

Well, as it turned out with each step I took into that big beautiful historic home, I was in complete awe! I was sold; now all my mom and I had to do was convince my husband. We couldn't get home fast enough to take him through the house. We were all in amazement, and before you knew it, we were the proud owners of this beautiful craftsman Dutch Colonial. Mom sold her house on La Flora, we sold our house on Magnolia, and we were all one big happy family, under the same roof.

Before closing, we did the much-needed walk through, as we had many questions about the property. As the prior owner was outside showing us the irrigation, we all heard a loud "boom" come from the inside of the residence.

I shifted my focus from listening and turned towards the home. "What was that - there is no one in the house?"

It wasn't just the loud noise we all heard, but the stillness we felt when a gust of the wind blew straight through our bodies. Very nonchalantly, the prior owner said, "Oh, not to worry that is probably Elizabeth."

Present picture of Redlands home, 2017

"Who is Elizabeth?" I queried.

"That's the ghost, don't worry though, Elizabeth is a friendly ghost."

"WHAT! What do you mean a ghost? You're kidding, right?"

"No, why would I kid about something like that?" At this point, we all stood there in bewilderment, and our hearts just seemed to drop into our stomachs.

"Really . . . did I just hear you correctly, are you telling us the day before closing there is a ghost in this house?"

"Yeah, but again, as I said, she is fine, she doesn't cause any problems, and you all don't have anything to worry about."

The realtors were with us, and they were just as stunned as we were. Why would anyone want to buy a house with a ghost? The seller did not disclose there was a presence lurking about the house. As you can imagine this new found information raised eyebrows, and nevertheless, nowhere in the listing was there a box marked "haunted!"

In my mind all of us needed clarification. No matter what anyone believes when it comes to spirits and the afterlife, this dwelling had more unexplained activity than any other house we had lived in over the years. We were all dumbfounded and had many more questions for the prior owner.

"How do you know for sure that there is a ghost in this house?"

"Well, we have lived here for twenty-five years, and in that time, we have never had a bad encounter with her. We have seen her a few times. She wears a blue dress and has long brown hair, and she is mostly active at night."

"Why do you call her Elizabeth, is that a name you gave her or does that name have any significance?"

"Elizabeth is the name of a girl who fell down the stairs to her death here many years ago; I assume it is her."

Considering this surprising revelation, the realtors realized if we were going to move forward that a declaration of facts needed to be drawn up making us aware there was a ghost living in this house. We were all a little leery, but that did not stop us from closing the deal on the house. We loved it, and the prior owner seemed to put our minds at ease that she was indeed a friendly ghost and meant no harm. Despite this new revelation, Mom was more than determined to move into this house.

There was one thing the prior owner was right about, as the unexplained activity seemed to ramp up at night, just when you're trying to get some sleep. We did experience unknown oddities that were questionable, and if we had not been made aware of the fact that a ghost lies in wait in the halls of this house, we would have been left in wonderment. Any strange noise we heard we would always attribute it to Elizabeth.

When we first moved in and were doing some of the renovations, we had several workers in the house. What I am about to tell you did happen, and to this day it is unexplainable. An electrician was installing new light fixtures, and another worker was installing carpet on the third floor. The rest of us were on the main floor unpacking boxes; suddenly, we heard a loud crash. It sounded like glass shattering on the ceramic floor. We all stopped what we were doing, and everyone ran to the second-floor landing.

"What the hell was that, did one of you break something?" Mom yelled as she ran up the stairs.

"No, we were wondering if you all might have broken something."

We all started looking around for any signs of broken glass; we found nothing until one of the workers began shouting, "Come look!" We went to where he stood, frozen, looking up and down repeatedly. He was standing in the doorway of the shared bathroom on the second floor. The light fixture the electrician just installed was sitting in the middle of the floor, intact. We looked at each other in complete disbelief; the ceilings in the house were at least ten feet high. There was no possible way for the fixture to fall and land on that ceramic floor and not shatter; it was seemingly impossible.

To this day, we think back on that incident and still scratch our heads and wonder what actually happened. There is no way it was our imagination as it wasn't just me; Mom and my husband heard the noise, the electrician and the carpet installer were there, and they heard it as well; we were stumped. The conclusion we finally came to was that this was our first encounter with Elizabeth. She must have caught the fixture and saved it from breaking; this was our explanation, and we stuck with it.

On another unexplainable event, my husband and I were fast asleep. My eyes opened abruptly at 3:00 am. I straightened up in bed, as I was suddenly struck with a waft of Frito-Lay corn chips that filled the house with a pungent, savory odor of Mexican food. The aroma didn't affect my husband at all, as he was snoring away until I began pushing him. Mom must not have smelled that strange scent, as she never woke up either; she slept right through the whole episode.

"Wake up . . . wake up!" I frantically whispered in my husband's ear.

He woke up to the sounds of my trembling voice, immediately sent chills down his spine. He jumped up and said, "What . . . what is wrong with you?"

It took a minute, but he finally smelled it too "What's going on? Is your mom in the kitchen?"

"I don't know, you tell me; I am too damn scared to get out of bed and look. You get up and see; Mom doesn't cook in the middle of the night. Do you think it could be Elizabeth?"

"Hell, I don't know."

We wished we had a bat or weapon stashed nearby. We got up, and I stood vigilantly near our bedroom door as I watched my husband slowly slither down the stairs and with each step, you could hear the weird cracking noise from the wooden floor. As soon as his foot stepped off the stair and onto the main floor, the scent completely disappeared; it was gone just like that. He flipped the light switch on in the kitchen, and there was nothing and no one to be found. Not sure if it was Elizabeth, but one thing is certain, we both smelled that unexplainable fragrance at 3:00 am that freaky night.

It has been said; that ghosts are most active at 3:00 in the morning. I don't know why. On another occasion, while Mom was asleep, she was awakened by a loud buzzing noise coming from her alarm clock at 3:00 in the morning. She rolled over, looked at the clock, thinking it was time to get up and got to work. She rubbed her eyes trying to focus in on the clock, and thought to herself, "I didn't set my clock radio for 3:00 am; I know I set it for 5:00 am." She sat up on the edge of the bed, wondering if Elizabeth had reset her alarm. Mom flipped the light switch on, reset the alarm for 5:00 am, and blamed Elizabeth for the 3:00 am wake up call.

Although there were many instances where we all encountered Elizabeth, another memorable event happened when Auntie Barb was visiting. She really hoped she would meet Elizabeth after all the stories she had heard. On her last night, she began talking out loud to her as if she were present in the room,

"Elizabeth this is my final night before I have to go home, I hope you come and see me before I leave."

Auntie Barb was lying down getting herself settled in for the evening. She heard the doorknob open, thinking it was Carly sneaking into Mom's bedroom to get in bed with her.

"Carly, is that you?" Auntie Barb whispered.

There was no answer. She lay there motionless. Could this be Elizabeth, she thought to herself. A few minutes passed; she mustered up the courage to check the door. Slowly she walked over to the door, she grabbed the knob pulling it securely shut and immediately dashed back to bed.

Auntie Barb was beginning to doze off to sleep; again, the door swung open. At this point, her pulse was racing, "It's nothing," she tried to tell herself; "it's just my imagination." Then she heard a floorboard creak as if someone were walking in the room; she froze, she couldn't breathe.

"Elizabeth, if that is you, I'm too scared to look and see!" she muttered.

She could feel her presence. At that moment, Auntie Barb got her wish; Elizabeth came to see her before she left. The next morning, she couldn't wait to tell my mom and all of us of her brief encounter with the mysterious Elizabeth.

We all lived in the house for approximately three years until my job transferred me to Orange County. Mom was not up for moving to Orange County; the cost of housing was a significant factor in her decision, and when she made her mind up, there was no changing it. Mom decided to move near my sister and her family in Texas; she was amazed at the kind of home she was able to get with her money there.

Joni was on to the next chapter in her life; her best friend, Barbara flew out and helped her make the long drive to Texas with Rattigan, her Devon Rex cat. He also made the trip from Illinois to California; he was accompanying her yet again on another adventure. Mom and Auntie Barb had so many funny stories about that road trip and the cat; one story Auntie Barb told me will always stick in my head. Rattigan was almost left behind; Mom had him all set up in the back seat where he had a cozy bed along with his food and water. The backseat had a car seat divider that folded down so he had access to the trunk, where his litter box was set up. Auntie Barb and my mom stopped to get gas and a bite to eat. They left Rattigan in the car locked up—at least that's what they thought. They came out of the restaurant and got back in the car; when Mom started the car, Barbara's voice was drowned out by the music on the radio.

"Hey, Joni, look over there, that cat looks like Rattigan."

Mom turned down the radio,

"Oh yeah, you're right, it does look a lot like him."

She proceeded to pull out of the parking lot and got a closer look at the cat; it was Rattigan! That darn cat must have slipped out of the car when they went inside to the restaurant. The whole time they were eating, they had no idea he was out pussyfooting around. Mom said she never stopped so abruptly before in her life. Auntie Barb quickly jumped out of the car and scooped up the cat. She was so thankful that nothing happened to him or even worse; she could have lost him forever.

In 2003, Mother was officially a Texan. She bought a beautiful new home in The Woodlands, Texas. Her boxes had arrived at the house before she did; Connie graciously unpacked the much-needed kitchen and bedroom boxes. When Mom and Auntie Barb finally arrived, they had a bed to sleep in and a functional kitchen. Once again, she would rearrange and redecorate.

Although I was incredibly sad to see her go, it was something I knew she could not be talked out of; she looked forward to living near Connie and her family. I realize now this was an unbelievable opportunity for my mother to be able to get closer to her other grandchildren, Bree and Brach. They loved having their "Noni" living close by. When Bree was little, she heard people call my mom Joni. She couldn't pronounce the "J" in her name, so she nicknamed her Noni, and it stuck.

As usual, she didn't stray from her calling; she quickly found a job working in a nearby hospital, Memorial Hermann in The Woodlands. Mom was loved there as she was at every facility she was employed. Not only were the doctors impressed with her nursing skills, but the CEO was amazed at her strong spirited, confident, and focused attention to help patients through the healing process as well as educating the newly graduated nurses; she was recognized for her services and named nurse of the year.

Mom met a new friend, Linda Becker. Although Linda was younger than my mom, they became good friends and spent most of their spare time together. If I had to describe Mom's personality, it would be summed up with the following adjectives: ambitious, courageous, gregarious, intelligent, extroverted,

Joni (left) Auntie Barb (right)

talkative, upbeat, and sympathetic. All great characteristics in making the best nurse ever. Now, anyone who has had the pleasure of knowing Joni I think would all agree that she was outspoken and never thought anyone could match that. Well, Linda surpassed that, and I think even Mom was taken back a bit by her funny and over-the-top outgoing personality.

Since Mom was single and didn't have a significant other to accompany her at her annual Christmas parties, Connie automatically became her plus two dates. They would go out with Linda, and she introduced them to chocolate martinis. They loved those deliciously sinful cocktails, call it what you will, as these are not your typical martinis; it is a "Drink from Heaven." That was just a primer before they would go to the party, and between Mom's and Linda's big bold personalities they would make a grand entrance.

Mom was happy living near Connie and her family. Family meant everything to her; however, in 2006 she was unable to deal with the heat, humidity, or the taxes in Texas, so she decided to move. The question was, at this point, to where. She had proposed going back to her roots and relocate to Pennsylvania to be near her best friend, but Connie and I were not very keen on the idea and for good reasons.

We knew Mom was aging, and if she needed Connie or me, it would be a bit more challenging for one of us to get to her. Mom had planned a trip to come out and see my family and me. While she was staying with us, we all went on a road trip to Prescott, Arizona. She had heard that this was a great retirement area and wanted to see it for herself. We were not there for more than a day, and she made her mind up that she would officially retire in Prescott. Mom would complain to my sister about the heat, humidity, and taxes that Texas had to offer; however, she didn't tell her that she wanted to move. When Mom returned from her trip visiting my family and me, she began packing and did not tell Connie. Much to their surprise, Bree and Brach had been visiting and noticed a bunch of packed boxes in her garage.

They didn't question Noni, but when they got home, they spilled the beans and told their mother. "We think Noni is planning on moving."

"Why, what would give you that idea?"

"Well, we saw a bunch of packed up boxes in her garage."

The cat was out of the bag; although this bit of news was surprising, it wasn't. My sister had her suspicions but wasn't quite sure what was up Mom's sleeve. I mean who decides to make such life-altering decisions on a whim, I ask myself, but for my mom, and the answer is just that—Joni!

Off she went once again and moved to Prescott Valley, Arizona. It wasn't what you call ideal for my sister and me. She spent only two and a half years in The Woodlands, but in that short time she would see the fallout of Hurricane Katrina and Hurricane Rita. They all hunkered down together as a family during that period.

Connie helped drive her out west. I know she was sad to see her go, but this trip would prove to be an excellent opportunity for mother-daughter bonding time. When they arrived, Mom wasted no time in unpacking. Prescott Valley became her home. She was surrounded by wonderful neighbors, and having such friendly neighbors that my mom could count on would put my sister's mind, as well as mine, at ease. What a blessing, as they seemed to all look after one another.

Mother was only seven hours by car and a quick flight from me if I needed to get to her. A life-long Lutheran, Mom found her way to a nearby church called Emmanuel Lutheran.

"From the very moment that I walked into that church, I felt that this would be where I would settle."

This church would become part of her family along with the neighbors that she met. Once again, true to her destiny and calling, she would go to work at Yavapai Regional Medical Center. Then later she would take a position at Mountain Valley Regional Rehabilitation Hospital where her years of experience and wisdom merged into a knowing and a caring for people of "unmatchable service." She settled into this beautiful little community for ten years.

We would make quite a few trips to visit her, and she planned trips to see my sister and her family as well. For the most part, she was happy and content with her life, outside of having to cope with arthritis. Mom had rheumatoid arthritis and osteoarthritis, but neither diagnosis seemed to slow her down until she reached her seventies, and even then, she worked until she was seventy-seven years old.

Throughout the years, she would travel with us on our family vacations. We went to Treasure Island, Florida, Cancun, Mexico, Padre Island, Texas, on a Royal Caribbean cruise, the Upper Peninsula, Michigan, on a Hawaiian cruise, and on many California side trips. She even surprised me at my wedding when I eloped to Las Vegas.

I have so many fond memories that run through my head, some good and some not so good, but what stands out the most is when I decided to leave the small town of Danville and head west to sunny Southern California. I was around the age of twenty-three. My life just wasn't going my way, and I needed a change. I moved to Long Beach, California on a whim. I recall the day I pulled out of the driveway; it was a tearful moment saying goodbye to my mom. I thought she would try to talk me out of leaving, but she didn't. She knew I had to carry out my dream. Whatever that was at that moment, I didn't know. I left almost everything behind and packed my clothes in garbage bags.

Three months in and I was ready to admit defeat. I finally found a job, but the living situation wasn't going well until one day I met two wonderful individuals, Danny and Bernie, who would change my destiny. I remain friends with Danny today. I was incredibly homesick, and I wanted to go home. I remember calling my mom and as a mother myself, now looking back, I am not so sure I could have been as strong as she was telling me to stay put. "There is nothing here in Danville for you. You have a job, and you can make it, I know you can. Don't give up, hang tough, you hear me."

"But, I miss everyone, and I want to come home!"

"You need to give yourself at least a year to adjust, and if you still want to come home, I will support your decision."

I am not so sure I would be strong enough to tell either one of my kids what she said to me at that time. To this day, I admire her strong will and encouragement to stay in California and tough it out. I would not have met my husband, and my life would have certainly taken an entirely different turn. We all must make decisions in our lifetime, but it is always nice to have someone help you along the way. Some things in life are black or white and so easy to make decisions. I am thankful she told me that day to stay put, even though I knew it had to be difficult for her as well.

So much in life is ambiguous, sometimes both decisions might be right or wrong, but if we wait for absolute certainty before acting, then we may never act. Reflecting back on that day, having my mom give me her words of wisdom made it much simpler in making that life-altering decision and as a result, it made me a better person.

Chapter 16

Goodbye Mommy

On December 14, 2015, I received an unexpected phone call before dawn. It was around 3:30 am. Startled and blurry eyed, I jumped up out of bed to see who was on the other end of the phone. I didn't recognize the phone number, so I didn't answer it. Then a few minutes passed, and the phone rang again. It was the same phone number. The question was who could be calling me at this time of the morning? My mind was getting ahead of itself, and scary thoughts were racing through it. At this point, I was fully awake and becoming a bit anxious. I quickly dialed my husband, who at the time was getting off his night shift and on his way home.

As I was talking to him, the phone rang again. This time it was Prescott's area code, and I instantly got a lump in the back of my throat; I knew it had to be Mom. Sadly, it was the emergency room physician at Yavapai Regional Medical Center explaining to me my mom was sick. My mind fogged over, as I was trying to keep my emotions together until that first tear broke free and the rest followed in an unbroken stream. My head was pounding, and my eyes were red and puffy from crying. I simply had to get to her. This news didn't make any sense to me, as I just talked with her the day prior. She was so happy and full of excitement as she was getting ready to go to a Christmas party. I think one of the toughest parts of life is the fear of losing a loved one. Was this her time? "Hello, is this Candy?"

"Yes, this is she."

"I'm not sure how to tell you, but your mother is very ill."

"What do you mean, how sick, she is going to be all right, isn't she?"

"Unfortunately, I am not sure, but what I can tell you is that we cannot treat your mother and we need your authorization to transfer her to Barrow Neurological Institute in Phoenix."

"She is going to make it, right?" I was sobbing uncontrollably at this point.

"I think she will make it down the mountain, but we believe she had an aneurysm, and she needs to be seen by a specialist."

"I will get to her as quick as I can."

I could barely think straight and called my sister within minutes after I received the news. We were on the earliest flights we could get. The ambulance transferred my mother to Barrow in Phoenix. I managed to hold my composure and get on a plane. The travel time although short seemed to last forever and was excruciatingly painful. The thought of not making it to her in time was just one of the many thoughts running through my head. When the plane landed, I raced to get in line to hail a taxi. I was lucky to get such a sympathetic cab driver, and when I told him my mom was in intensive care, he quickly rushed me to the front entrance of the hospital in hopes that I would make it to her in time; he was so kind.

When I arrived, they were running all sorts of tests on her. The nurse tending to my mom had me sign for some of her personal belongings, as she was wearing a gold bracelet. They also gave me some of her hair that they shaved, as they had to insert a shunt to relieve some of the pressure off her brain. Seeing her in that hospital bed for the first time hooked up to tubes and wires was a shock to me. She looked so deflated. She was completely out of it and didn't even appear to be the same person; I was not prepared for that. Then again how could anyone ever be ready to see either one of their parents that ill? Mom's diagnosis was Arteriovenous Malformation (AVM) in her neck region.

I sat with my head lowered holding her hand waiting for Connie; she was a welcome sight when I looked up and saw her walking towards me. We hugged each other not sure what the next couple of weeks would hold for us. I often wonder if a guardian angel was watching over my sister and me that day; as what are the odds of the hundreds of taxis that filter through the airport that Connie would get the same taxi driver? She did! I'm certain my Grandma Doyle was guiding both of us.

I remember when we met the neurosurgeon for the first time; he explained to us what had occurred. It was startling and overwhelming. Normally, arteries carry blood containing oxygen from the heart to the brain, and veins carry blood with less oxygen away from the brain and back to the heart. In Mom's case, unfortunately, her veins were a tangle of blood vessels, sort of like tangled yarn. Therefore, the blood from the arteries to the veins didn't flow properly, causing them to burst and bleed into the brain.

The question was could this be repaired; with therapy and rehabilitation, would my mom be able to get around and care for herself? The answer that her surgeon gave us was, "Yes, it can be repaired, but the following ten days post-surgery will be a testament to her surviving. We have to take one day at a time and go from there."

Essentially, what that meant to me was that she had a 50/50 chance. Mom couldn't have ended up in a better hospital. She had one of the most renowned neurosurgeons in the country; there was no question, she was in good hands. It was all up to her.

The days following her surgery were challenging; the doctor was able to repair her AVM, and Mom fought the good fight. For the next two weeks Connie and I didn't leave her side, we stayed at a nearby hotel. Both my sister and I felt it was a shame there wasn't a Family House available for us to stay at during our mother's hospitalization.

The next couple of weeks were tough on Mom and extremely emotional for my sister and me. It was Christmas time, and we were praying that she would pull through the holidays, "tis the season," it was challenging for everyone. Oddly, that was probably the first year Mom didn't make plans to come and visit one of us. She proposed driving to my house, but I refused to let her. In my opinion, and both Connie and Auntie Barb agreed, it was out of the question as it was too far and we were concerned for her well-being. We tried to get her to fly, but her stubbornness got in the way, and she decided against it. Connie had just sold her house in Texas, and as usual, my husband was working so we couldn't get away. The plan was that my family and I would see her in February, as we were going to tour Northern Arizona University. Mom was campaigning heavily for Carly to attend NAU; she was excited to think that her youngest granddaughter would only be a little over an hour away. As I sit here and reflect on that day, it reminds me that even the best laid out strategies don't always go as planned.

Throughout her stay in the hospital, the nurses were comforting not only to my sister and me, but most importantly, to Mom. The hospital was a teaching institute. Each day the neurosurgeon would make his rounds with the residents, and every day we would ask, "Do you think she is going to make it?" He would not falter from what he initially told us, "One day at a time."

Connie and I began making phone calls to her friends and family. For some, it was just too far for them to come and visit, but her Prescott friends came and saw her. I think the hardest part was seeing her in pain, not to mention seeing her on a ventilator. Although she was under sedation, she knew her surroundings. Due to her AVM, she had to be awakened to follow commands from her nurses; for example, she was asked to move her fingers, feet, hands, and arms. Typically, she would pass with excellence despite the weakness on her left side. Mom seemed to be progressing after the surgery.

When she was awake, she would talk to us by using her fingertip to press against the palm of our hand spelling out words. Sometimes it was hard to decipher, but for the most part, we were communicating. She told us both over and over how much she loved us. She even asked us to get her some ice cream. There's love for food and love for desserts, and then there's Mom's love for ice cream. Mom truly loved her ice cream. I wish we could have given her some, but it was against the doctor's orders.

It was December 23, 2015, and the doctors felt Mom was doing well enough to be extubated. It was a calm day but a scary one at best. My mom had her affairs in order, and she did not want any heroic measures taken. She also made it clear to us that if she couldn't go home and care for herself and her dog to let her go; hearing those words in that exact moment broke my heart, I couldn't imagine my life without her.

Before the doctor began prepping to remove the breathing tube, he spoke to Mom, "Joni, you seem stable, so we are going to take out your breathing tube. I know you have a directive not to resuscitate, but there is a chance that you may struggle to breathe and we must reinsert your breathing tube." Her eyes widened as he asked her this question, "Are you OK with me reinserting the breathing tube if you are struggling to breathe?" She nodded her head yes.

Quite a few healthcare workers were surrounding her as they took out the tube. On the count of three, they removed the tube. I was waiting in the hall near her room. Within a matter of minutes, she began to labor. She was gasping for air. The team quickly jumped into action and reinserted her breathing tube. I couldn't hold back the tears; at that moment, my heart broke. The doctor then informed us that he would try removing the breathing tube in a couple of days.

Mom seemed to be doing better but what she was fighting was now pneumonia. She was getting antibiotics intravenously, but she didn't appear to be getting any better. I feared the possibility of her not recovering from pneumonia. My mom was a registered nurse and understood what had happened, and she realized the implications. She was being suctioned regularly but needed a tracheotomy. She made it clear to us that she didn't want to undergo this procedure.

It was Christmas Eve, and she was resting comfortably. Connie and I were hoping she would be strong enough on Christmas Day, but the doctors were hesitant. We stayed by her side, rubbed her legs and feet, doing whatever we could to make her comfortable. Mom wanted us to take a much-needed break and get away from the hospital. We were invited to spend Christmas Eve and Christmas Day with some dear friends that lived in the nearby town of Chandler. We knew if anyone could make us laugh, it would be none other than Brad Blissit. Mom was acquainted with both Holly and Brad, and when we told her we were invited to go, a tiny smile emerged from her face in approval.

That didn't mean we didn't spend time with her, as we did. I feel like those last few days we spent with her through the holidays were a gift to us, as she expressed her love in ways that are unexplainable. I suppose, in a sense, the much-needed time would allow us to come to grips with the possibility of letting her go.

The day after Christmas, we showed up; the look on her nurse's face was not good. Apparently, overnight they were slowly weaning her off the sedative and the recent x-rays they took off her esophagus; showed some paralysis. She should have been fighting the tube, and she wasn't. It was time to say goodbye, but how do you say goodbye to someone that you love so dearly?

All I wanted for her was to ensure that she was kept comfortable and didn't have to suffer throughout this procedure. My family members had been there the week prior spending time with her. Devin is, and was, special to my mom in a way that she couldn't quite explain. Not that she loved any of her other grandchildren differently because she loved them with all her heart. Devin is an image of Danny boy. She had a mural painted of the two of them side by side. She used to tell me she felt like God was giving her a second chance to see what Danny might have looked like if he would have lived.

Devin decided he wanted to make the drive and be by her side the day we all agreed to take Mom off life support. If there was ever a time when he stepped up to the plate, it was those last couple of days that Mom was with us. Devin did not leave her side. I am confident Mom knew he was with her.

We all talked to her as much as we could until they made sure the sedation took full effect so she would not endure any pain. We called family and her closest and dearest friends so she could hear their voices one last time. It was finally time for the healthcare providers to remove the tube. Connie and I had been through a similar experience with our dad; we knew what to expect. It's just that part of me always wondered what if the doctors are wrong and she very well might survive and breathe on her own?

Since the life support was a mechanical respirator and made certain noises, there was silence when they turned it off. Suddenly there were no loud buzzers; it was quite peaceful. The room was full of anticipation of when she might take her last breath. It was the calm after a tornado that surrounded us by the visual display of destruction. This kind of thick silence usually chilled me; that day the silence caressed my heart, soothing my soul that soon, Mom would be at peace.

Her respirations began to slow down, but she didn't stop breathing within minutes as we all thought would happen. The doctor told us it could be minutes, hours, or days before she would pass. After a few hours of her breathing on her own, we decided to transfer Mom to the hospital's hospice care where we would stay by her side for the last couple of days of her life. Devin spent the entire night with her, and she survived through the first night. He chattered to her most of the evening, reminiscing about the fun times he shared with her growing up.

By far the hardest part was the waiting, and no one knew when she might take her last breath. We were so worried if we left her side that she would die alone. If there was one thing I remember, it was my mom telling me that she didn't want to die alone. On the other hand, the hospice doctor said that in some cases loved ones don't want you to see them take their last breath. He explained to us that over the years, he witnessed family members that stood vigilant at their loved one's bedside, and when they stepped away they let go.

It was now December 28, 2015, and although the doctor had shared that bit of information with us, we so desperately wanted to be near her holding her hand, stroking her hair in hopes to give her solace. We stayed the entire day and most of the evening. Devin once again, would not leave her side. He told us he would call us if there were any change. Connie and I needed to sleep, as these past two weeks were draining, to say the least. We knew we could get to her fast, as we were less than a few minutes away, right across the street.

I finally settled in bed and started to doze, and suddenly the phone awakened me. It was Devin, "Mom, I think Grandma may have just taken her last breath." I flew out of bed grabbed my pants and jacket. "Are you sure, did you tell the nurses?"

"No, I haven't alerted the nurses yet, I called you first as promised."

"Ok, I'm hanging up and calling Aunt Connie, alert her nurse. We will be there in a flash."

I called Connie, who was on the same floor in the hotel. We made it down the elevator together, and as we were running across the street, she accidentally pocket dialed her husband, Skip. He could hear us frantically racing to get to our mother. We got there, and I am sure she could sense we were there. We collapsed over her, hugged her, and said goodbye.

She died on December 29, 2015, several minutes past the midnight hour; she was gone. Grandpa Doyle wrote so many tender letters, one of which I came across several years ago when I was helping Mom write this story. I discovered the note in the pile of pictures and letters Mom tucked away safely in a lockbox. This time when I reread the note, I found it to be particularly significant as it contained much more meaning. I am not sure if Mom was sending me a message, but the date when Grandpa wrote the letter is the same year my mother was born. The day and month he wrote the letter was the exact date she left this world to move on to be with her loved ones in heaven.

This being the 29th day of Dec
the year of Our Lord 1936 - and
being in Good Health, Sound
of mind and Body I here by
Grant and Will - all my earthly
belongings both Real and
Personal to my Wife Dorothy
Ann Dayle.
And it is my Wish to be laid
to Rest at Petersville Oh. in the
Family Lot that my Wife will
select. D. Frank Dayle

He was forever thinking of his beloved Dorothy and daughter Joni. Love to you in the skies!

As hard as it was letting her go, we knew it was what she wanted. She was finally at peace and with her parents and her precious Danny boy. Her two-week long journey in the hospital finally ended. Mom, being the nurse that she was, donated her body to science.

It's hard to believe that I find myself sitting here writing these final words on Christmas Day, 2016, wondering what it is like to cross over to the other side. My mom always believed that her mother was her guardian angel and fiercely watched over her. I would like to think that my mom is also a guardian angel watching over my sister and our families, as well as me.

I don't believe for a minute my mother was scared, as she was ready. Mom planned her funeral. It may seem morbid to some people, but for her, she wanted to make sure we did not have to make any difficult decisions regarding her funeral arrangements. She left instructions to us in a letter.

"I don't want either of you to worry. I know I will be with Jesus and I will be united in my spirit, I am sure, with all my loved ones. I will always be with each of you; all you have to do is call on me, and I will send my blessings to you and your angel forever. I love you both with all my heart. You both have always made me proud. I adore my son-in-laws and my grandchildren. Be strong during my wake. I trust that as hard as it might be to give a eulogy, you must be strong."

That was just a few words in her letter to my sister and me. She also had left behind an attached envelope that read, "Open this at the time of my death. Both of you should be present—Mom."

In that envelope, she outlined, specifically, how she wanted her personal belongings to be divided. With each word I read, crocodile tears fell onto the paper. I wiped the tears from my face while reading her final words and I felt her presence. It was just like her to give us a bit of a tongue-lashing even after her passing. Her last words were, "If you and your sister cannot agree to the terms that I have outlined for each of you, sell everything and split the cash."

I will be forever grateful in her careful planning in preparing what was considered one of the hardest days for my sister and me. Her final wish was, upon her cremation when we had the time, to take her back to Danville, Illinois, to put her remains at rest beside her son.

Mom also had written out poems and hymns to be read at her funeral in Prescott. She lived her last ten years out in the town where she touched so many people and made a slew of friends. That day the house of God was packed with her friends and family; and, oh yes, because of Mom's final wishes, Joni would have the most beautiful send off to heaven. Through her encouragement, Connie and I stood firm; we got up in front of the congregation and gave a eulogy and we are confident she would have given her approval.

The following summer, we traveled back to Danville and arrived at the cemetery where Mom would lay to rest. It was a beautiful sunny day, with the birds chirping, on July 30, 2016. Everywhere I looked, there were so many reminders of when we buried our father. I had not been to that cemetery since he passed away on March 27, 2004. It was a simple service lead by her dear friend and boss for twenty-nine years, Dr. Bill. All of her family was there, and many of her close friends came to say goodbye.

Devin and Bree read poems as Mom requested, and the hymns she chose played in the background. As we placed her urn in the box before it was lowered into the ground, I shed a tear in both sadness and happiness knowing she was at her final resting place.

My mom was everything to my sister and me. Her smile and warmth lit the world around her with so much love. Most of all, her faith was undeniable as she was ready for the Lord to take her. I could never prepare for my mother's death, and letting her go was just as challenging as it was for me to say goodbye; I know she is at peace. She had always felt a strong connection to her mother who took her in when she was just an infant. I want to say thank you not only to my Grandma Doyle but also to my mom for being an amazing and inspiring woman to all who knew her. I know she left the world better than she found it. Her legacy will live on for many generations because of her sweet and beautiful heart.

Final Thoughts from Candace

Who would have thought that I could have ever written a book in my lifetime? I am a true testament that through determination and perseverance you can do anything if you set your mind to it. With each word, it gave me comfort knowing that I was carrying out my mother's wishes to complete her story. Remembering all those years ago, when my mom came to me with the idea to tell her personal life story about how Iva handed her over to strangers on a street corner. I struggled with the thought of ever getting it done.

It is my hope you have enjoyed reading this book as much as I did in composing it. I wrote it not only to communicate with the hearts of those who at birth have been abandoned, but also to give hope to those adopted or fostered, for it can indeed be a blessing. I also confess that authoring *Blessed to Be Unwanted* helped me to understand what my mother endured as a child growing up. Naturally, she often wondered about her biological parents as well as her foster parents. Although, as much as I wish my mother were still beside me, I now know that her passing is what gave me the strength and courage to forge forward and finish this body of work.

My dearest mother is my guardian angel. I can feel her looking over me and guiding my path each day. I can envision her big beautiful smile peeking down from the heavens above. Sharing her story was her final wish, and I know she is beaming with happiness that it is finally happening. Above all Mom's life experiences inspired me to share the following points with you.

7 Things to Consider While Fostering or Adopting a Child:

1. Have Unconditional Love: One must be willing to put their life on the line without any guarantee or expectation he or she will return their love.

2. Be Informed and Aware: You don't have to be wealthy or own your home to adopt or foster a child. However, an important factor that comes to mind is to ensure that you are familiar with all Family Child Care Home licensing laws and regulations.

3. Characteristics Needed to be a Good Foster or Adoptive Parent: Being loving, flexible, stable, and most of all dependable. My grandparents were real advocates for children; with each child they cared for, they showed no discrimination.

4. Know the Risks: Understand while you are a foster parent caring for a child, it is important to "stay in the moment" and to give him or her the love and attention needed. Grandma knew the risk that at any time Joni's biological mother could return to claim her. Therefore, it was important to cherish every day she had with Joni, no matter what!

5. Create a Support Team: My grandparents quickly learned that it was important to surround themselves with a network of support. For those of us who have had children or adopted a child, I think we have all heard the quote, "It takes a village to raise a child." In the beginning, Dorothy thought she could handle taking on any number of kids, although she quickly learned

they needed to acquire help. Not just emotional support, but also logistical, i.e., clothes, food, and toys.

6. Being a foster parent isn't for everyone. You must be willing to sacrifice your freedoms. As a parent to two beautiful children I never stop parenting, even though they have left the nest. When fostering you must be able to let go; typically, when someone agrees to foster a child such as my grandmother did, you live with the thought of their biological parent returning. Agreeing to foster a child in need is the ultimate sacrifice any one person can make; however, we can't forget about a precious life that will be forever grateful for the love and care you provide.

7. A Message to Unwed Mothers: Joni's birth mother was at a crossroads in her life and she ran away to have her; it is important not to be afraid to ask for help. Some facilities can assist women who are facing an unexpected pregnancy. Today many more options allow women to have their child in a safe place. Once again, the Safe Haven Baby Box is a way to provide a safe way to surrender your newborn without fear of criminal prosecution.

It is my hope to hear from you. I invite you to visit me at www.candacewebbhenderson.com and share your story and feedback. You can also reach me at candy@candacewebbhenderson.com. May you and those who love you always be blessed.

With Love,
Candace Webb-Henderson
www.candacewebbhenderson.com

Special Tributes to
our Heroine Grandma Doyle

To an amazing grandmother who showed every person she
encountered compassion, generosity, and serenity. I remember
sitting on the front porch with her. She would talk to anybody
who walked by and often had a smile for everyone. Grandma
Doyle played a big part in my twin sister's and my childhood.
I can remember times sitting in her kitchen and tasting the
dishes that she prepared with so much love. She taught me the
true meaning of what it means to be part of a family. Thank you,
Grandma Doyle, for taking in my mother all those years ago, as
there is no greater blessing than the love of a mom. Every day I
am thankful for the years I had with her and you. It's her example
I look to as I mother my children. Here's to both of you!
—Your Loving Granddaughter and Daughter, Connie Sue

Mrs. Doyle: I remember Joan once told me that I was the only
one allowed in the basement apartment where you and your
loving husband lived. That made me feel special, but then you
always had a way of making people feel loved. I never thanked
you for taking Joan in as your daughter because you and I never
discussed that subject. I wish I had because if you hadn't opened
your heart to her, I would never have met my dearest and best
friend. You always called us "kiddos." Well, this kiddo thanks you
from the bottom of her heart.
—Love to all, Auntie Barb

My first encounter with Mrs. Doyle was in 1979 while working as an investment broker with Pittsburgh-based Moore, Leonard, and Lynch, a firm founded in 1877. Her neighbor, Helen Nalepa, referred Mrs. Doyle to me to assist her with some investments. After forty-four years in the business, I still recall Dorothy Doyle as an extraordinarily happy lady. We spoke numerous times by phone, and I always enjoyed hearing her melodious voice. Through the years, in addition to discussing investments and the financial markets, she also frequently spoke to me about her family and interests. Our conversations were always a delightful experience because of her optimistic outlook on life and her joyful anticipation of the future.

—Herb Zehnder, Vice President, Wealth Management,
UBS Financial Services, Inc.

About Candace Webb-Henderson

Born in Danville, Illinois, Candace Webb-Henderson followed
in the same footsteps as her
beloved mother, Joan Doyle
Webb, and her grandmother,
Dorothy Burr Doyle, working
in the medical industry helping
others. Her greatest inspiration
was her mom signing words
in the palm of her hand on her
death bed. She told Candace to
complete the book, *Blessed to Be
Unwanted*. Not only did she tell
her to finish *Blessed to Be Unwanted*, she asked for her favorite
food, spelling out "ice-cream."

Praises for *Blessed to Be Unwanted*

Candace Henderson's *Blessed to Be Unwanted* is an extraordinary testament to how her mother transformed tragedy into a triumph of the human spirit and now, through Candace, delivers a remarkable message to adoptive and foster children about their limitless potential for fulfilling their life purpose. I highly recommend this book as well to foster and adoptive parents.
—Michael Bernard Beckwith, author of *Spiritual Liberation*

Candace's book really touches on the core and the heart of adoption. Her humble and gentle views really connect you to her. Reading her life stories and how she uses every lesson to learn and grow, is something everyone can relate to in every age, and aspect of life. Her book is a "must-read" for any family contemplating fostering or adopting.
—Priscilla Pruitt, Mrs. International 2016 / Spokesperson for Safe Haven Baby Boxes

Candace Henderson has done with her story what most people can never find their way to and that is empowering those that have no voice. Those that quietly suffer inside wondering who, what and why their lives were the way it was. She takes what would be a bad experience and makes it something for all to learn from. Bravo and a job well done and definitely a must-read.
—Daniel Gutierrez, Best-Selling Author/ Global Speaker/ Spiritual Teacher/Master Business/Life Coach/Philosopher / www.danielgutierrez.com

Blessed to Be Unwanted is a heartwarming story of a family's love for a child abandoned shortly after birth. Candace Henderson delivers an inspirational story of how one woman's devotion changed a child's destiny. This book is a testament to the potential in every human life and is a must-read for anyone considering fostering or adopting a child.
—Joe Tanner, Retired NASA Astronaut

Candace Henderson has written a magnificent story involving adopted love through three generations. Her mother and I had much in common. I, too was abandoned at birth and adopted two years later. *Blessed to Be Unwanted* is a must-read for anyone planning an adoption.
—Burton F. Gustafson, former Special Teams Coach, Green Bay Packers

This book has you hanging on to every word as this family works through the devastation of abandonment. It is a must-read!
—Monica Kelsey, founder of Safe Haven Baby Boxes

Made in the USA
Coppell, TX
15 September 2020